Land and People

Land and People

Land Uses and Population Change in North
West Connemara in the 19th century

Eibhlín Ní Scannláin

Connemara West Plc.
and Connemara National Park, Dúchas The Heritage Service.

CONTENTS

LIST OF PLATES

LIST OF FIGURES

Eibhlín Ní Scannláin studied at NUI Galway and after obtaining her B.A. in Geography she went on to successfully complete her M.A. with the Department of Geography in 1988. Her joint contribution to an essay entitled 'North-West Connemara; Processes and Patterns of Landscape Change in The Nineteenth Century' was published in Decoding the Landscape, Collins, T.(ed) 1994 (reprint 1997).

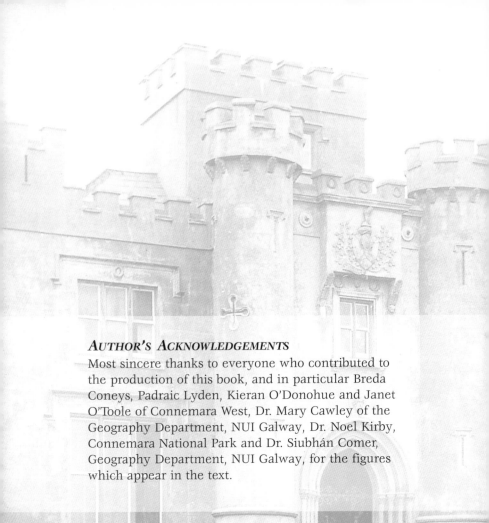

AUTHOR'S ACKNOWLEDGEMENTS
Most sincere thanks to everyone who contributed to the production of this book, and in particular Breda Coneys, Padraic Lyden, Kieran O'Donohue and Janet O'Toole of Connemara West, Dr. Mary Cawley of the Geography Department, NUI Galway, Dr. Noel Kirby, Connemara National Park and Dr. Siubhán Comer, Geography Department, NUI Galway, for the figures which appear in the text.

Editorial Group Acknowledgements

We would like to acknowledge with thanks the following who assisted us with this publication: Joan Johnson, Waterford, Michael Gibbons, Clifden, The National Library, The National Archives, The Illustrated London News Picture Library, The Ordnance Survey Office, The Religious Society of Friends; and Galway Rural Development for their financial support.

THE IRISH FAMINE OF THE mid 19th century was a catastrophe and a turning point in modern Irish history and much has been written about its causes, course and consequences.

North Connemara was no exception in terms of the ravages to population and great individual pain and suffering which are part of the famine story. Although the Great Hunger was a national catastrophe, each county or district or community had its own story and experiences and the folk memory of these experiences have their own shape and flavour in each community to this day

Eibhlín Ní Scannláin is to be congratulated for taking a studied interest in the famine in North West Connemara and especially in giving us valuable information about the context in which it happened and some of its notable consequences. This book is based on Eileen's post-graduate research during the late 1980s in NUI Galway which she has developed and updated for this publication. The text gives graphic accounts of the tragedy and of the immediate and medium-term effects it had on the population of the North West Connemara area and especially on how the pattern of landholding and farming was forever changed from that time.

We know from other accounts of the famine that alongside the scale of this human tragedy there also existed bureaucratic malaise, government ineptitude and the indifference or greed of fellow human beings who, by fortune or wealth, managed to insulate themselves from the social devastation around them. But, as Eileen's work shows, the tragedy also stirred individuals, a few landlords and small groups who, motivated by compassion and religious or humanitarian convictions, plunged themselves into efforts to help the population regain their physical strength and self-respect. The story of James & Mary Ellis in the 1850's and of Sophia Sturge three decades later (all of whom worked in Letterfrack) are examples of remarkable people whose commitments and achievements are extraordinary, even by today's standards. These were people who were not just interested in the immediate alleviation of distress but in re-building the capacity of people to stand tall again and to have faith in the power of community service and co-operation to provide a better social and economic future for themselves, for their neighbours and for their children, or at least for those of them who had not died or emigrated.

The legacy of such people was greater than they could have imagined. It exists still in the houses they built, the trees they planted and even the fuschia bushes which now grow so abundantly in our area. Perhaps other research will soon examine if their efforts could also be credited with sewing the early seeds for the success of many community and development initiatives which have been the hallmark of the area in the final decades of the 20th century.

For now, however, Eileen's book is a valuable and timely reminder of not just the work of such people but also of the dramatic changes which took place before and particularly after the famine in the North West Connemara region especially in relation to land and people. Eileen's work shows that the latter half of the century saw the extension and development of roads, the building of bridges and harbours and the laying down of the relatively short-lived railway from Galway to Clifden. This is the story of the beginnings of the social and economic development of North West Connemara and as such is the framework within which we all live and work today.

This is not just the story of people long dead – it is also our story for these people were our ancestors and our predecessors. It is with pride and pleasure therefore that we in Connemara West and Connemara National Park (both occupying today the buildings and lands of James & Mary Ellis) have been able to bring this story to publication as our gesture to marking the 150th anniversary of the famine.

Kieran O'Donohue
Connemara West on behalf of the Editorial Group
Mary Cawley
Breda Coneys
Noel Kirby
Padraic Lyden

This work is based on the author's M. A. thesis entitled "Athrú Tírdhreacha i bPáirc Náisiúnta Chonamara agus an Cheantair Máguaird ó Thús an Naoú Céad Déag", 1988. (Unpublished). NUIG.

INTRODUCTION

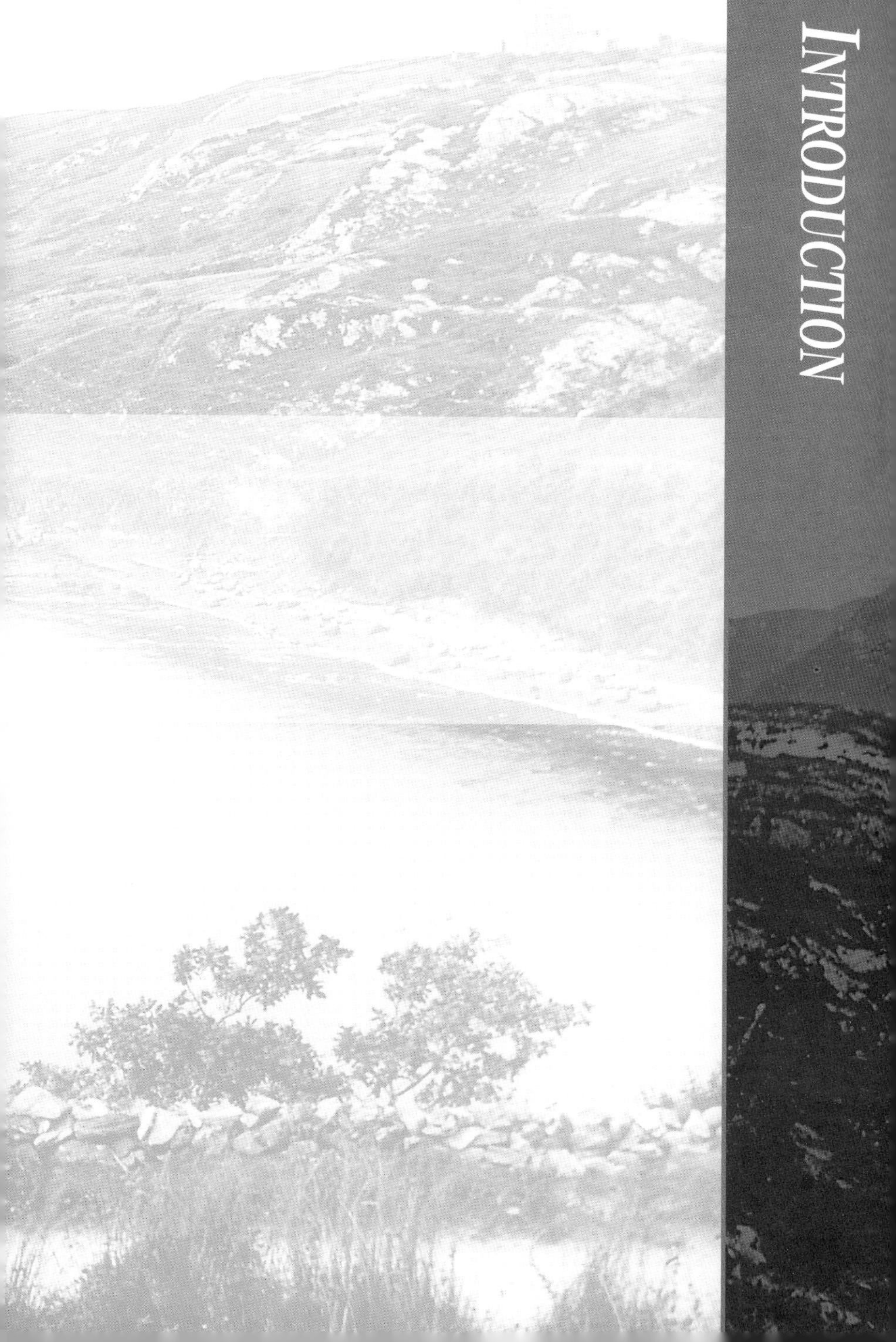

The area of north west county Galway covered by this book broadly encompasses the District Electoral Divisions (D.E.Ds.) of Ballynakill, Bencorr, Cleggan, Cushkillary and Renvyle. It forms part of the region known as Iar Connacht. Population and agricultural statistics referred to in the study relate to the Barony of Ballynahinch, Clifden Union and the D.E.Ds., depending on their availability.

The area's landscape is largely a product of the process of glaciation which carved the mountains of the Twelve Bens which form the eastern boundary of the study area. From the Twelve Bens, deep valleys covered with thin stony soils and vast tracts of blanket bog, interspersed with lakes and streams, extend northward to Killary Harbour and westward to the Atlantic seaboard. To the south, the main Galway to Clifden road forms the boundary (Fig. 1).

The west of Ireland in general, and the western seaboard in particular, remained largely isolated from the mainstream of national economic life during the 1800s. Iar Connacht's isolation was due in part to distance from the main market centres, poor communication networks and general transport difficulties. Changes such as land enclosure, the reorganisation of the *clachan* form of settlement and the commercialization of agriculture generally occurred much earlier in the east of Ireland than in the west. During the early nineteenth century the population practised a subsistence economy, largely dependent on the produce of their small holdings, which in many cases had to be supplemented by other sources of income.

Road construction schemes, financed by Parliamentary grants from 1822 onwards, and the extension of the Midland Great Western Railway from Galway to Clifden in the 1890s were undertaken largely as relief measures to sustain the population. Together with transport improvements, the development and establishment of market centres, including the town of Clifden, contributed to agricultural development, increased trade and the integration of the area's subsistence economy into the national economic system.

The major social and economic changes which occurred in Ireland as a whole in the mid-nineteenth century are generally traceable to the Great Famine years. In the area of north west Co. Galway, prior to the catastrophe of the crop failure of 1847, the population was already distressed due to previous crop failures and to a lack of capital investment by landlords or Government. Population decline commenced on a substantial scale during the 1840s and continued into the twentieth century. The assistance provided in the form of food and employment by the Religious Society of Friends and by some landlords, during the famine, did much to ease the population's destitution and assisted in development.

During the post-famine period, the transfer of land proprietorship from the landlords to former tenants was facilitated by various Land Acts between 1870 and 1923. This resulted in an increase in the total number and size of medium-size holdings in areas such as Clifden Union making farming a more viable enterprise. Livestock production increased in importance and sheep rearing emerged as the main agricultural enterprise in upland areas of west Galway from the mid 1800s.

At the close of the nineteenth century, north west Galway had a better road network and had improved forms of transport, including a regular train service from Galway to Clifden. The area's inhabitants for the most part became the owners of their holdings. Tourism at this point was also an important enterprise as is evident from the very favourable comments on the area's natural beauty in various travel guides.

Together with the Great Famine, the area's location and physical landscape appear to have been most influential in creating what is present-day Iar Connacht. The Great Famine served in many ways as a watershed in the social and economic history of Iar Connacht. The first part of the text examines living conditions in north west Co. Galway prior to the Great Famine. The second part explores the impact of the famine on the area and the means of alleviation employed by the government, local landlords and the Religious Society of Friends. The final part looks at the consequences of the famine and the development of Iar Connacht as the twentieth century approached.

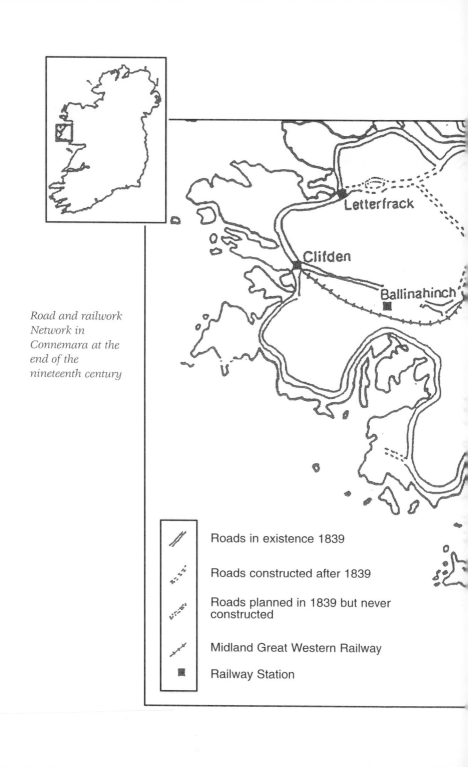

Road and railwork
Network in
Connemara at the
end of the
nineteenth century

Letterfrack

Clifden

Ballinahinch

Roads in existence 1839

Roads constructed after 1839

Roads planned in 1839 but never
constructed

Midland Great Western Railway

Railway Station

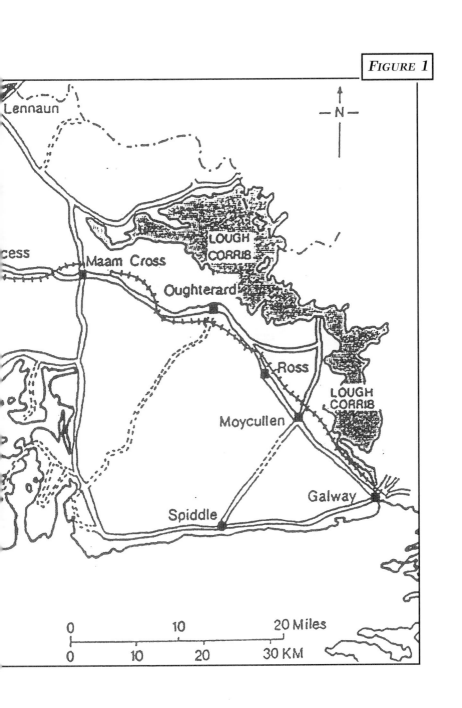

FIGURE 1

PART 1 PRE FAMINE IAR CONNACHT

POPULATION

The Irish population, including that of north west Galway, increased rapidly during the latter half of the eighteenth and the first half of the nineteenth centuries. Increases in population of 68% and 20%, were experienced between the years 1781 - 1821 and 1821 - 1841, respectively, at a national level (1). Population increase was particularly marked among the labourer and small farmer sectors who were concentrated along the west coast in counties Donegal, Mayo, Galway, in the south west in counties Kerry and Cork and in mountainous areas in the east, such as Wicklow (2). The increase in population has been attributed to the eagerness of landlords to subdivide property (particularly following the enfranchisement of Catholic 40s. freeholders in 1793) and the abundance of potatoes which 'was the mainstay of a diet ... it tended to prolong life by lowering the incidence of disease' (3).

Pre-famine Iar Connacht was primarily a rural area with a large and increasing agricultural population. The population consisted of two main classes during this period: (i) the landlords such as the Martins of Ballynahinch, D'Arcys of Clifden, Blakes of Renvyle and the Thompsons of Salruck; and (ii) their tenants and labourers who represented the majority of the population. Clifden, founded in 1822 by John D'Arcy, was the area's main port and market centre (4). The Barony of Ballynahinch, in 1821, contained a population of 19,408 and, by 1841, this number had increased by 72% to 33,465. By this time, living conditions were already distressed due to food shortages experienced throughout the early nineteenth century, the competitive demands on a diminishing amount of available arable land, the absence of resident landlords and their agents, and the limited employment opportunities available to a rapidly increasing population. Potato yields were reduced in Co. Galway, during the years 1801, 1807, 1816, 1821, 1831 1839 and 1842 due to various reasons such as drought, heavy rainfall and storms (5). In *Letters from the Irish Highlands of Cunnemara*, first published in 1825, a member of the Blake family of Renvyle described conditions in Letterfrack and its environs as follows: 'The

straggling village of Letterfrack is situated in a rocky district
... But of what avail can it be to look for improvement
where there is no resident landlord? In every rood of
ground you trace the absence of a fostering hand while the
miserable cabins, falling in ruins around you, repeat the
same melancholy tale' (6). Samuel Lewis, author of the well
known *Topographical Dictionary*, was in the vicinity of
Ballynakill shortly after the failure of the crop in 1831, and
reported that the inhabitants were 'reduced to the greatest
distress' - some 1,500 families would have perished, in his
view, but for the relief afforded (7). It is clear from these
accounts that a large portion of the population was
experiencing great distress prior to the Great Famine. The
main employment avenues pursued by the population of
north west Galway at this time were in agriculture, but, due
to poor returns from farming, incomes in many cases were
supplemented by fishing, kelp making, illicit distillation,
domestic industries, marble quarrying and relief works
organised during periods of distress.

AGRICULTURE

As in many western rural societies, agriculture formed the
main source of employment in rural Ireland during the pre-
famine period. Poor communication networks, as indicated
by the Taylor and Skinner road maps of 1778, isolated Iar
Connacht from much of the remainder of Ireland, thus
keeping its population largely self-sufficient. Large scale
road building and improvement did not take place until
parliamentary grants were made available for this purpose
in 1822. Therefore, during the pre-famine period,
communication in north west Galway was essentially by
sea or by bridle paths. Accordingly, pastoral farming
continued to be the chief agricultural enterprise in Iar
Connacht during the late eighteenth and early nineteenth
centuries with some limited tillage consisting mainly of
potatoes and oats. In 1791, Coquebert de Montbert visited
Connaught and reported that only one tenth of the province
was tilled (8). Hely Dutton who conducted A S*tatistical and
Agricultural Survey of the County of Galway* for the Royal
Dublin Society in the early 1800s, found that 'almost the

entire of the Baronies of Ballynahinch, Ross and Moycullen is pasture'(9). These reports suggest that the change from pastoralism to commercialised tillage farming which took place in Irish agriculture more generally during the second half of the eighteenth century did not reach the more remote areas of the west until much later.

Owing to Britian's involvement in the Napoleonic Wars (1803-1815), the demand for Irish corn was greatly increased in the early nineteenth century. This resulted in reduced livestock prices and was reflected at local market level. Hely Dutton found that in Co. Galway 'in 1807 cattle were uncommonly cheap, and a universal slaughter of calves and young cattle took place' (10). The consequence was that in three years the prices rose. 'The graziers, however, have no right to complain; they have generally become purchasers of land' (11). Cattle prices were to fall again in the 1820s. 'The great fall in the price of cattle and sheep at Ballinasloe, in October 1820, spread a general gloom over the province of Connaught; the prices for cattle were from three to five pounds each less than last year' (12).

Most small farmers in north west Galway kept a few sheep for the purpose of wool production for domestic use. The weaving and knitting of wool were the main domestic enterprises. Any surplus produced supplied the local markets during the early nineteenth century as Hely Dutton observed '... in Cunnamara a very considerable quantity, indeed I believe the whole, is worked up in stockings of which there is a very considerable sale. There may be some flannel and frizes (sic.) made but I imagine not much. The genius of the women seems to lean to knitting stockings, which only wants encouragement to make them superior to any in the world for the same price; the usual retail price of the pedlars is twenty pence per pair' (13). During the early nineteenth century, £10,000 worth of stockings were knit in Connemara and sold in towns and villages such as Clifden and Tullycross. While cattle prices were in decline at this time, Hely Dutton reported that the price of sheep increased and that 'wool sells now (in 1815) for 26s. per stone. In 1819 it rose to 32s. per stone but in 1820 it fell to 20s.' Sheep were also making from 10-15 shillings less per head at this time (14).

Footnote: 240d (Pennies) = 20s (shillings) = £1 pre decimal.

LAND OWNERSHIP

As the mid-nineteenth century approached and livestock production became established as the chief agricultural enterprise, it was realised that more land was necessary for its successful operation and that it was a less labour intensive practice. The combination of these factors resulted in evictions, emigration, migration within the island and some consolidation of holdings. Due to the limited availability of land, an ever increasing population and generally high rents, subdivision of holdings became a widespread practice among tenant farmers during the late eighteenth and early nineteenth centuries. Three main factors were involved in promoting and supporting subdivision. In 1784, Foster's Corn Laws were passed under which a bounty was paid on the export of grain from Ireland, thus increasing the price of Irish grain. Grain cultivation, being labour intensive and requiring but small holdings to produce good and profitable yields, resulted in a large number of small farms supporting a rapidly increasing population. As it was in the landlord's political interest to have a large number of freeholders on the rent roll, particularly following 1793, unrestricted subdivision of holdings followed on a large scale. In order to ease the competition for the rapidly declining amount of agricultural land available and to support an increasing agricultural population, it was necessary to subdivide existing holdings and to cultivate marginal land (15).

Subdivision was practised in the west on poor quality land for the most part and was associated with a subsistence economy. It appears to have been less prevalent in areas of commercial farming such as east Connacht and the east of Ireland in general (16). Subdivision was severely restricted after Catholic Emancipation in 1828 and the increase in voting qualification valuation to £10 per annum in 1829 (17). General Alexander Thompson of Salruck, in his evidence to the Devon Commission in 1845, stated that though he had resettled over two hundred families on marginal lands, subdivision still prevailed. 'They are so fond of subdividing that their holdings will not support the number of people that creep in upon them. Their object is to make the rent out of the fishery and to support the family out of the potatoes.'(18)   The Rev. John Griffin, who was Parish Priest at Ballynakill, said that it was 'prohibited generally but still in operation ... subletting is practised unknown to the landlord, (He was referring to the estate of Mr. Francis Graham of Ballynakill) (19).

The method of holding land most prevalent among the tenant farmers of the west, during the late eighteenth and early nineteenth centuries, was rundale. It was regarded as the fairest way in which to divide various soil qualities and other natural amenities among struggling small farmers. Rundale, according to R. H. Buchanan, 'had five main components: common arable or infield, an outfield used for pasture and periodic cultivation, common meadow, rough grazing which usually included peat bog and small enclosures near the farms for gardens and haggards' (20). In 1839, when Francis John Graham purchased his property at Ballynakill, 'It had been for a great many years, twenty or thirty years under the courts, and without a landlord; ... it was covered with paupers; it was underlet; the houses like Indian wigwams, and without fences, while the mountain part, which was very good in other respects was quite uninhabited. ... When I got the property it was in running dale: twenty families upon five acres of ground' (21).

The practice of booleying or transhumance was frequently associated with rundale and survived only in the more remote parts of Ireland into the nineteenth century. Booleying involved the movement of livestock to mountain pastures during the crop-growing season (May-October) and the building of temporary dwellings known as *brácaí* in Connemara, to provide shelter for the herders (22).   The only traces of the practice in today's agriculture are the commonage rights held by farmers to rough grazing pastures adjacent to each townland.   These commonages were divided among the land owners in each townland by a measure of collop. 'One scale was 1 collop = 1 full grown cow = 3 year old stirks = 8 sheep = 8 goats = 20 geese, but local variations existed'(23).

The clachan form of settlement was closely associated with rundale. The tenant farmers who lived in this kind of social nucleus formed a co-operative system of ploughing, cultivating, harvesting, turf cutting, sharing of draught animals, harness, farm implements. They also shared various soil types and other natural amenities (24). In Co. Galway, as J. Mannion pointed out, the *clachan* form of settlement was more prominent on limestone based soils in east Galway and along the shore between Galway city and Inverin in the south (25). Some clustered settlements also existed during the first half of the nineteenth century in the north west as seen on the 1839 edition of the 6" O.S. maps. For instance, there was a *clachan* consisting of eighteen buildings in Addergoole townland (Fig. 2) . The decline of rundale, booleying and of the *clachans* was brought about by the inability of progressively smaller holdings to support their population, the enclosure and reclamation of wastelands, the consolidation of holdings particularly after the famine, and the development of roads which encouraged settlement in a ribbon pattern (26).

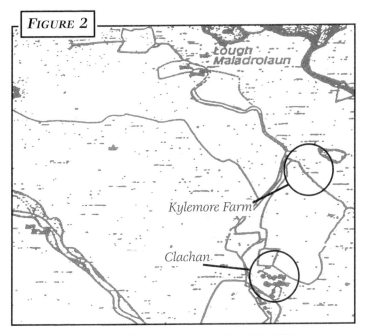

FIGURE 2

Clachan settlement, Addergoole townland (O.S. 23", 1839)

Based on Ordnance Survey Ireland by permission of the Government permit No. 6798 © Government of Ireland (O.S. '23)

PLATE 1

Dawrosbeg, Letterfrack - Lazybeds.
Courtesy of the National Library of Ireland.

LAND RECLAMATION

Due to Iar Connacht's dependence on agriculture for economic viability, the improvement of farming practices and particularly land reclamation were priorities among landowners. The Scottish engineer Alexander Nimmo, was appointed in 1814 to enquire into the nature and extent of the bogs west of Lough Corrib and the practicability of draining and cultivating them (27). He found the area of Iar Connacht to be 'one of the most uncultivated parts of Ireland. On a general view indeed, it seems one continual tract of bogland and mountain. The greatest disadvantage is the want of roads, of which there is not one in the whole district fit for a wheel carriage, nor is there a single bridge'(28).

In pre-famine Ireland, the tenant farmers appear to have been the chief wasteland reclaimers. In his report, Nimmo remarked on the reclamation of some 1,000 acres by a member of the O'Flaherty family at Renvyle, by removing 'the cottagers from their old stations and settled them on the bog: this they reclaimed with potatoes and seaweed, treating it afterwards with the sand of the shore, which contains calcareous matter, the effect has been very great' (29). In this report, Nimmo also mentioned that 'at the head of Ballynakill there is a flat about 1,000 acres on which some attempts have been made at drainage' (30). Rev. John Griffin of Ballynakill, in evidence to the Devon Commission in 1845, said landlords encouraged their tenants to improve their holdings by letting 'at a low rent- say 5s. an acre; 7s. 6d. or 10s. the mountain part of it' (31). Charles Samuel Cooper Esq., Surveyor, also in evidence to the Devon Commission 1845, reported 'the last time I was there (Ballynakill) I could perceive a very considerable advance in the reclamation of land' (32).

To prepare the land for cultivation the tenant farmers constructed ridges and furrows known as lazybeds. This technique was used to drain the land and enabled them to grow potatoes, oats and flax on dry ridges (Plate 1). The method of constructing the ridges varied throughout the country. In Galway during the early nineteenth century, Hely Dutton wrote that 'Potatoes are usually planted in ridges of about six feet broad, the furrow about three feet' (33). Lazybeds were generally spade constructed in line with the slope for maximum drainage. A few gentlemen cultivated in drills. The lazybed technique was widespread during the eighteenth and nineteenth centuries due to 'the recognition of their usefulness in breaking in wasteland for cultivation' (34). These reclamation works were facilitated by the local availability of 'extensive banks of calcareous sand round the coast in almost every bay and in the interior are numerous beds of limestone' (35). which were used to fertilize the newly reclaimed lands. Prior to the discovery of limestone on some properties in the district, for instance on the D'Arcy Estate, lime was occasionally made of '... large beds of oyster shells ...' (36). 'Once land was reclaimed and drained, however, the need for high ridges diminished' (37). This resulted in the decline in widespread ridge cultivation towards the end of the nineteenth century. Its decline was also affected by the introduction of advanced agricultural implements and machinery. Surviving traces of lazybeds bear testimony to former occupancy.

FISHING

Despite north west Galway's considerable stretch of seashore, the fishing industry was not a key source of employment for its population. Fishing was practised on a part-time basis, largely to supplement agricultural income. This lack of development was due in the main to poor and unsafe piers and harbours, some bad fishing seasons in the early nineteenth century, and the lack of available capital to facilitate the purchase of boats and the fishing tackle necessary. Projects such as the construction of piers at Roundstone, Cleggan, Ballynakill and Derryinver were commenced to create employment in times of distress during the first half of the nineteenth century. Their building was first supervised by Alexander Nimmo, and by the Irish Board of Public Works after 1832. In many cases, completion took a long time as Henry Blake's account of the pier at Ballynakill depicts: 'Ballynakill is one of the harbours where during the scarcity of last year (1823), a pier was begun under Mr. Nimmo's superintendence. It afforded some employment to the poor at the time but the work is now stopped, and so little has yet been done, that we could hardly, among the surrounding rocks, distinguish the spot' (38).

Inland fisheries, such as the salmon fishery at Ballynahinch, were very important to the region. George Preston White visited Ballynahinch fishery in the late 1840s, which was leased and directed by Mr. Robertson of Derryadda Lodge. Mr. Robertson was also the London Law Life Assurance Company's agent on the Martin Estate at Ballynahinch. He had 'done much good in this desolate part of the country and gives considerable employment in his salmon fishery, and also in his extensive establishment for preserving provisions' (39). General Thompson built a smoking house at Salrock where he also established a village for his employees. By 1846, the Hon. David Plunkett had applied for permission to build a smoking house at the head of Killary Harbour. This was granted later. Among other major land owners in Iar Connacht to apply to the Public Works for grants either to build or improve piers and quays were F.J. Graham, Ballynakill (landing slip and wharf), A.Thompson, Rosroe (quay and landing slip), J.A. O'Neill, Bunowen (a pier) and Thomas Martin, Roundstone (repairs to the existing pier) (40). Further attempts were made by the Religious Society of Friends during the famine and later by the Congested Districts Board (C.D.B.) to establish a successful fishing industry in the region (41).

LOCAL INDUSTRIES

Kelp making was a thriving industry on the north west Galway shores during the late eighteenth and early nineteenth centuries. It 'became a considerable business among shore dwellers in the eighteenth century as the growth of the industry stimulated the production of soap, bleaching materials and glass' (42). At first, kelp (which was the name given to burnt seaweed) was burned for use as fertilizer on the land, but following the intervention of Scottish dealers it became an export industry. The burning of the seaweed was carried out mainly by cottagers or small tenant farmers near the coast (43).

In the initial stages of the industry, the black weed was burned because it produced soda for which there was a good market in the late eighteenth and early nineteenth centuries. The quantity of black weed kelp manufactured in Iar Connacht in the early 1800s amounted to 4,000 tons per annum (for which 50,000 tons of seaweed were necessary). Its cost, including cutting and burning varied from £1.10s. to £2 per ton and by the early 1820s a ton of kelp sold at under £4. Prior to the famine its price increased to £15-£20 a ton. This high point was short-lived due to the discovery of a cheaper method of producing soda by le Blanc and subsequently the black weed kelp industry declined and by 1869 its value had dropped to between £1 10s. and £2 10s. a ton (44). Alexander Nimmo noted that 'Kelp in 1808 sold in Galway at £13 per ton ... at present the price is so low as £3 10s. to £4 so that many of the farmers find it more for their interest to employ the weed in agriculture' (45). Consequently, a new industry based on red weed kelp was introduced and developed by a Scot named William Patterson of Glasgow. The industry was established to obtain iodine and the price of kelp varied in accordance with its iodine content (46). Prices ranged from £3 - £5 a ton. In the 1860s, an average of 2,500 tons of red weed kelp were exported from Iar Connacht and purchased by a Scottish firm (47).

As kelp making was a small farmer's occupation, the cutting of the weed commenced after the tillage was completed in April or May. The weed was collected by hooks into boats or baskets and landed on good gravel beaches. These beaches were considered best for the process of drying and burning. If the beach was sandy the sand adhered to the weed and reduced its sale value as it added to its weight and decomposed the iodine compounds. The kilns used in burning the weed were built of loose stones on the beaches. They were about 'eight feet long, three wide and eighteen inches high, the 'eye' of the kiln being placed opposite the wind to catch the draft' (48). Hely Dutton reported that a considerable amount of kelp making was carried out in the Renvyle area, as did the C.D.B. inspectors in the 1880s and early 1900s. Mrs. Blake of Renvyle House and Mr. Burke of Clifden gave an account of its practice in their evidence to the Board. Mrs. Blake said she held a 'royalty of 12s. 6d a ton... no matter what the price of kelp' on kelp made of weed collected off her land and rocks (49).

Illicit distillation was another important source of income for the small farmer or labourer. Following the re-introduction of excise duty on Irish spirits in 1661, the 'struggle between 'parliament' whiskey and poteen' was resumed (50). The practice of illicit distillation reached its highest point during the late eighteenth and early nineteenth centuries. Prior to the famine it was seen by many as their only chance of survival. It supplemented farm income and enabled tenants to pay their rent. In Galway some landlords are reputed to have 'commonly accepted poteen in lieu of rent' (51). At the beginning of the 1800s, malt was the main source of pulp used in the distillation process but later an abundance of cereal crops, largely due to a decline in market demand following the conclusion of the Napoleonic Wars in 1815, encouraged the use of raw grain. During the 1860s, molasses was substituted for these. H. D. Inglis who wrote a travel book entitled *A Journey Throughout Ireland during the Spring, Summer and Autumn of 1834*, found that illicit distillation was carried out openly and that the crop of barley sown after the potatoes were harvested was expended by the numerous private stills of Connemara (52).

The practice of poteen making started to decline prior to

the famine. From the *Fisheries Ireland Committee Report* published in 1849, and Mr. D'Arcy of Clifden's evidence to the Commissioners of Public Works in 1846, it is clear that a 'great deal' of poteen making went on prior to the construction of roads (53). The roads enabled members of the Revenue Police and the Royal Irish Constabulary to reach into once remote areas most likely to harbour poteen stills. These reports also confirm evidence given to the The Public Works Committee of 1830, in which it was stated that the introduction of Public Works to this area had contributed to the decline in poteen production (54). Changes in landownership, especially during the second half of the nineteenth century, also strongly influenced its decline. As an increasing number of tenants gained ownership of their holdings and, accordingly, had an 'assured source of income' in their farms, they were therefore less dependent on other sources of income (55).

The Connemara serpentine rock, better known as Connemara marble, is probably the most commercially valuable rock in Iar Connacht. Marble was quarried at a number of locations in west Galway: for instance, in the north west at Lissoughter; on the eastern shores of Derryclare Lough; on the south east of Cregg Hill, where a green marble quarry was operated; and, on its north western side, close to the Owenglin River where a white marble quarry was worked. Even during the first half of the nineteenth century, Inglis found that the marble quarries of Connemara afforded little employment and appeared to have been worked very little (56). Apart from the lack of roads and efficient transport facilities, the want of commercial development of these quarries was 'owing to the peculiarities of the marble, and the danger of destroying it in the operation of sawing' (57); and the absence of a market. Inglis found that Conemara marble was unpopular on both the English and Irish markets (58). In 1868, similar problems prevailed according to Rev. McManus in *Sketches of the Irish Highlands*. 'I may mention that before my first visit to this country, Mr. Martin, after attempting in vain to overcome the prejudices against it, as being Irish, got a ship-load of it sent to Italy and thence back again to England as Italian marble; by which it obtained a ready and lucrative sale' (59).

ROADS

Subsequent to 1822, when Parliamentary Grants were first made available for the purpose of road building in Ireland, many new roads were planned and existing paths or roads were improved or replaced. In 1832, a Board of Works was established in Ireland and part of its duty was to organise road works as a relief measure during periods of distress (60). Many of these roads, as those planned by Alexander Nimmo, remained unfinished for many years due to lack of funds and the problem of poor communications persisted. One road of major importance to the region of north west Galway, planned by Nimmo in the early nineteenth century, was that connecting Clifden and Westport through the Kylemore Valley. This eighteen mile portion of road from Clifden to the head of Killary was estimated to cost £2,880 (10s. per perch); bridges and sewers £1,400 (61).

In 1816, when John D'Arcy first went to live in Clifden he had great difficulty in riding a horse on the road from Galway 'but now in 1820 he is enabled to drive a coach and four horses in hand from Galway to Clifden. ... He is also now perfecting a new line of road from Clifden to Oughterard, which, instead of going over steep hills as at present, will run for nearly thirty miles with scarcely any difference in the level' (62). In 1822, Henry Blake took up residence at Renvyle and experienced similar difficulties. 'He brought over an English Broad Wheel Wagon and it was landed on the sea shore and could never be got further' (63). In 1840, for one 'to visit the district about Renvile - four miles north of the main road - he will require a stout horse and a strong car, for the 'path' now appertains to old Connemara' (64).

In 1834, Maria Edgeworth on her visit to Connemara found that a mile of Nimmo's road between Clifden and Leenane was uncompleted and was 'unpassable by man or horse or boy or Connemara pony' (65). In the 1840s Mr. D'Arcy of Clifden, in his evidence to the Commissioners of Public Works (Ireland), stated the Government had 'commenced several' roads 'none of which are as yet completed' (66). The 1839 O.S. 6" maps also provide evidence of the progress of road building in Ireland. For instance, between Letterfrack and Kylemore in 1839 there was a portion of unfinished road. Cartographic evidence confirms that the road to Leenane was planned to go north of Pollacappul Lough but in 1864, when Kylemore Castle was built, the road was diverted to the south (67) (Fig. 1).

However slight the communications improvements may have been during the first half of the nineteenth century, the Public Works Committee of 1830 stated, 'the effects produced by these public works appear to have been - extended cultivation, improved habits of industry, a better administration of justice, the re-establishment of peace and tranquility in disturbed districts, a domestic colonization of a population in excess in certain districts, a diminution of illicit distillation and a very considerable increase to the revenue' (68).

OVERVIEW

Overall, Iar Connacht prior to the famine was a predominantly agricultural area containing a large population of labourers and small farmers who, due to exorbitant rents charged on poor quality holdings, were compelled to engage in non agricultural enterprises to supplement their incomes. The population was already in a distressed state having experienced previous crop losses and little assistance was available to them. The level of proprietorship among small farmers at this time was very low. The subdivision of holdings and the rundale method of dividing land was commonplace in this area. The lack of appropriate communication networks limited access to markets and thus hindered the commercial development of the region's economy. The lack of adequate financial aid is reflected particularly during times of distress and in the many accounts given of relief works commenced but discontinued for this reason. Settlement was concentrated on the more fertile soils along the coast. While the coast line is expansive, kelp making appears to have been the main occupation of those occupying the shore line. Fishing was engaged in on a part time basis only, largely due to the unsafe nature of piers and harbours. Cattle and sheep production were the main agricultural enterprises with crops consisting chiefly of potatoes and oats.

Some aspects of rural life were improving, however slowly. Probably the most renowned changes to take place in Iar Connacht's landscape concerned attempts made at land reclamation. Whilst Alexander Nimmo organised drainage schemes, and some few landlords invested in improving the quality of their land, the main improvers appear to have been those unfortunates who found themselves removed from their holdings to rough ground on the pretext of low rents. This period also saw the foundation of an improved road network in north west Galway.

REFERENCES

1   D.B.Grigg, *Population Growth and Agrarian Change, a Historical Perspective* (Cambridge University Press 1980).

2   L.M. Cullen, *An Economic History of Ireland since 1660* (London 1972).

3   K.H. Connell, *The Population of Ireland 1750-1845* (Oxford 1950), p.161.

4   K. Villiers-Tuthill, *A History of Clifden 1810-1960* (Galway 1982); J.A. Lidwill, *A Seagrey House:The History of Renvyle House* (Galway 1986).

5   W.P. O'Brien, *The Great Famine in Ireland a retrospective of the fifty years 1845-95* (London 1896): *Galway Reader* Spring 1951,Vol.3 No.3.

6   Blake, *Letters from the Irish Highlands* (London 1825), p. 296-297.

7   S. Lewis, *A Topographical Dictionary of Ireland Vol. 11* (London 1847), p. 156.

8   S. Ní Chinnéide 'Conquebert de Montber's impressions of Galway City and   County in the year 1791' *J.G.A.H.S.* Vol XXV Nos.3 and 4 (1953-54), p. 1-14.

9   H. Dutton, *A Statistical and Historical Survey of the County of Galway with observations on the means of improvement* (R.D.S. 1824), p. 105.

10   Ibid., p.123.

11   Ibid., p.123.

12   Ibid., p.123

13   Ibid., p.145.

14   Ibid., p.123.

15   Grigg, op. cit.

16   Cullen, op. cit.

17   R. F. Foster, *Modern Ireland 1600-1972* (London 1989).

18   Devon Commission Vol. ll (1845), evidence no.491, p.467.

19   Ibid., evidence no. 492, p.469.

20   R.H. Buchanan, Field Systems of Ireland, in A.R.H. Baker and R.A. Butlin (eds.) *Studies of Field Systems of the British Isles* (London 1973), p. 586.

21   Devon Commission, op.cit., evidence no. 498, p,477.

22   J.M. Graham, 'Transhumance in Ireland with special reference to its bearing on the evolution of rural communities in the west', unpublished Ph.D. thesis, Queen's University Belfast (1954).

23   J.M. Graham, 'Rural Society in Connacht' in N.Stephens and R.E. Glasscock (eds.) *Irish Geographical Studies* (Belfast 1970), p. 20.

24   R.H. Buchanan, 'Rural Settlement in Ireland' in N. Stephens and R.E. Glasscock (eds.), *Irish Geographical Studies* (Belfast 1970), p. 146-161.

25   J.J. Mannion, *Landholding and Settlement in County Galway*, unpublished M.A. Thesis (N.U.I. 1964-65).

26   Ordnance Survey 1839 and 1864 eds.

27   A. Nimmo, *A Report on the Bogs in that Part of the County of Galway west of Lough Corrib, Appendix 12 to the fourth report of the Commissioners on the Bogs in Ireland* (1814).

28   Ibid., p. 191.
29   Ibid., p. 191
30   Ibid., p. 203.
31   Devon Commission, op. cit., evidence no. 492, p.468.
32   Ibid., evidence no.543.
33   Dutton, op.cit., p. 63.
34   J. Bell, A Contribution to the Study of Cultivation Ridges in
        Ireland in *J.R.S.A.I.* Vol.114 (1984),   90.
35   Nimmo, op.cit., p.188.
36   Dutton, op.cit., p. 36.
37   Bell, op.cit., p.94.
38   Blake, op.cit., p. 278.
39   G. Preston White, *A Tour in Connemara with remarks on
        its great physical capabilities* (London 1849), p. 22-23.
40   Public Works Ireland Fourth Report (1846).
41   C. Woodham Smith, *The Great Hunger* (London 1962):
        Congested Districts Board Reports Vol. x (1907).
42   E.E. Evans, *Irish Folkways* (London 1957), p. 219.
43   Dutton, op. cit.
44   G.H. Kinahan, The Seaweeds of Yar Connaught and
        their uses, *The Quarterly Journal of Science*, July (1869).
45   Nimmo, op.cit., p. 190.
46   Kinahan, op. cit.
47   Ibid.
48   Ibid., p. 335.
49   Congested Districts Board Reports, op.cit., p.275.
50   K.H. Connell, *Irish Peasant Society* (Oxford 1968), p. 1.
51   Ibid., 29.
52   H.D. Inglis *A Journey throughout Ireland during the
        Spring, Summer and Autumn of 1834* (London 1835).
53   *Fisheries Ireland Committee Report* 1849,(2020):
        Commissioners of Public Works 1846.
54   Reports to the Public Works Committee Report 1830
55   Connell (1968), op.cit., 46.
56   Inglis, op.cit.
57   Ibid., p. 76.
58   Ibid.
59   Rev. McManus, *Sketches of the Irish Highlands; descriptive,
        social and religious with special reference to the Irish
        mission in west Connaught since 1840* (Dublin 1863),
        p. 201.
60   L.M. Cullen, *The Emergence of Modern Ireland* (London
        1989) : Nimmo, op.cit.
61   Nimmo, op.cit., p. 203.
62   Dutton, op. cit., p.375.
63   M. Edgeworth, *Tour of Connemara and the Martins of
        Ballynahinch* (London 1950), p. 72.
64   Hall and Hall, Ireland, its Scenery, Character, etc. vol iii
        (London 1841), p. 487.
65   Edgeworth, op.cit., p.27.
66   Public Works Ireland Fourth Report (1846), p. 41.
67   6" Ordnance Survey Maps (1839, & 64 eds.) sheet 23.
68   Public Works Ireland, op. cit., p.43.

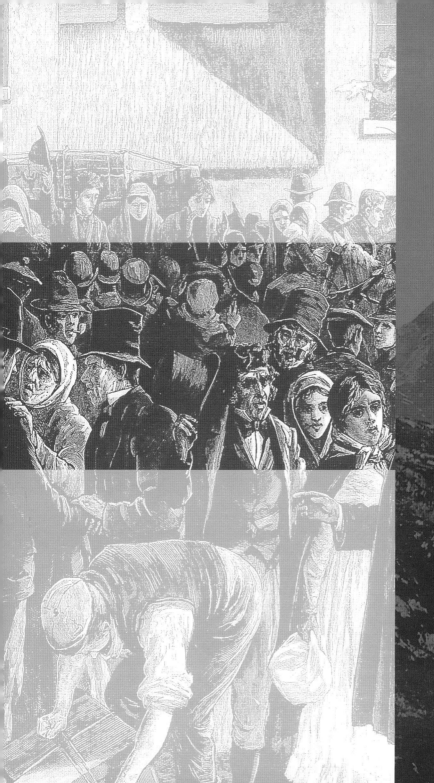

IAR CONNACHT DURING THE 1840s

Phytopthora infestans (a fungus commonly known as potato blight) first infected the potato crop in 1846 in limited areas but, in the autumn of 1847, practically the whole Irish potato crop was destroyed. This led to high mortality rates, largely due to starvation and its associated ailments, particularly in the west where the population was highly dependent on the potato for sustenance (1). In the east of Ireland, at this time, the population losses were largely due to emigration which 'was already substantial before 1846' (2). In the area of north west Galway, it was reported to the Devon Commission in 1845 by Mr. Mullins of Clifden (a shopkeeper) that 'The small tenantry and labourers are much on the decline, from the want of capital in the country. Neither public nor private work can be carried on, to afford the poor labourer who is pining away by the fireside a scanty 6d. a day for his day's work. The poor labourers hold their huts and gardens from the smaller farmers in general, and pay on an average yearly from £1 to £1. 10s. partly in work and partly in money' (3). The Rev. W. Flannely, who had been appointed curate in the Parish of Ballynakill eight months prior to the Commission's enquiry, reported that on visiting the Thompson property in Salrock they travelled 'through the whole of it, and cannot get a chair or stool to sit on, in the discharge of our duties, or a jug to take a drink of water from; and as for beds, it is dreadful, the people are stretched, not on straw, but on heath, the growth of the wild mountain' (4). Mr. Kearney of Clifden reported that the condition of the smaller tenantry and labourer in the district was 'miserable in the extreme: poor people cannot on an average, get three days work a week, probably not more than two and their wages are 6d. a day...' (5).

According to the Rev. W. Flannely, these conditions were attributable to the 'banishing of people from their holdings; from some districts, entire villages have been thrown on the world. In other cases I attribute it to paying high and enormous rents for their lands; for instance paying 50s. an acre for some portion of land that has been on account of their relative position by the sea, being a fishing country and where they have been depending upon the fishing, which has failed for the last three years principally'(6). Referring to rental arrangements among tenants on his own estate, General Thompson of Salrock, in evidence to the

PLATE 2

Clifden Workhouse
Courtesy of the National Library of Ireland

Devon Commission, reported that 'They have the mountains in common; the farms near the shore they divide ... most of them are tennants (sic) at will. ... I assist them to build houses. I have allowed them £5 to build houses and the first three years free of rent; then I allow them for making all the drains and all the fences and enclosures. Then after the fourth year I charge them 1s. an acre, and they go on til (sic) it goes to 10s. and not exceed 10s. for 21 years' (7).

In 1845, the Blake estate at Renvyle was reported by General Thompson to be the only estate in north west Galway on which rents were set by the acre 'and that is set at 30s. the Irish acre, but that is over the average of the county setting' (8). At this time, Mullins reported to the Devon Commission that 'proprietors have set their lands around the coast at a higher rate by setting those sunken and wild rocks in with the land;... the smaller farmers are debarred from getting manure, which in a great measure prevents them from tilling' (9). 'The rent is payable at May and November some by lease, and some by valuation. The sum is gross and not by the acre. The valuation of land was rather a novel thing here until within the last three or four years... Land averages now from 10s. to 15s. an acre- that is bog; rough reclaimable from £1- £1 10s.; arable £2 - £3' (10).

Due to the deterioration of living conditions in Ireland during the early nineteenth century, an Irish Poor Law Bill was passed in 1838 under which the country was divided into Poor Law Unions (11). One such Union was based on Clifden where a Union workhouse to accommodate 300 persons was built at a cost of £3,600; (fittings cost £900) (Plate 2). It was opened on March 8, 1847. 'In general, conditions in the workhouses were designed to be such that only dire necessity could drive a poor person to seek admission for himself or his family. Only the bare essentials were provided, with very few refinements; the atmosphere was one of penury' (12). As food availability decreased and prices soared following the winter of 1846, a Temporary Relief Act was introduced in June 1847. Under this Act soup kitchens were established to afford outdoor relief. It was expected at this time that the potato crop of 1847 would be abundant and that temporary relief measures would suffice until harvest time when work and food would be readily available once more (13). The Government ordered the Commissioners to scale down outdoor relief operations from August and to cease completely in September of 1847. The Government more or less considered the famine officially over at this point (14). In 1847, a Poor Law bill was passed but one of the main stipulations was the quarter-acre clause which meant that only those with less than quarter of an acre of land would receive assistance (15). This Act administered Irish famine relief from 1847 on. This led to further desertions and the consolidation of holdings. At this time, W.E. Forster, a member of the Religious Society of Friends, who visited areas of the west to furnish the Society's Relief Committee with a report on conditions, found that there 'is probably at the present time no portion of the community labouring under greater difficulties and provisions than those whose occupation of land exceeding one quarter of an acre has excluded them from poor-law relief, and who cling to their holdings as the only means of future subsistence' (16). His account of conditions experienced by the largest and most destitute sector of the community led to the establishment of soup kitchens in areas such as Cleggan and Salrock.

Potato blight, combined with the severe weather conditions experienced during the winter of 1847, led to high mortality rates, largely due to starvation and its associated illnesses, particularly in the west where the majority of the population consisted of tenants and labourers who were heavily dependent on the potato for sustenance. The number of persons in need of assistance also increased, leading to severe overcrowding in the workhouses (17). The inability of the official workhouses to accommodate the increasing number of destitute led to the establishment of fever hospitals and auxiliary workhouses in store buildings and deserted big houses. While travelling in the area in 1851, J.H. Ashworth, who visited the west of Ireland in search of settlement, had one such building adjacent to the Rev. Mr. Duncan's residence (now The Kylemore House Hotel) identified by his guide. This building had been used as a hospital and poorhouse during the famine. Relief stores were also established at Ungwee (on the Graham property) and in Renvyle in March of 1847 (18).

THE RELIGIOUS SOCIETY OF FRIENDS

During 1847, members of the Religious Society of Friends visited the west of Ireland to report to the Central Relief Committee on areas most acutely distressed and in need of assistance. In autumn of that year, James Hack Tuke visited Iar Connacht to find that the potato crop was almost consumed and that 'At least one quarter of the population of Connaught are at present existing upon these turnips or turnip tops, boiled with half decayed potatoes. On the sea coast they eke this miserable food with sea weed and sea-eels' (19). He reported that Clifden Union '... is bankrupt, and I found a few days prior to my visit, the wretched inmates of the poorhouse had been expelled and the doors closed. The estates which compose the Union of Clifden are ... mortgaged to nearly their full value' (20). Clifden Union workhouse and other such institutions were much reliant on financial aid collected as Poor Law Rate from the larger landowners of the Union, many of whom were absent, bankrupt and whose property was under the Courts. The Poor Law Bill of 1847 also decreed that landlords were responsible for the payment of rates on holdings of less than a quarter of an acre. Poor Rate collectors met with considerable hostility in north west Galway, as is evidenced in the Outrage Reports of this period. 'I have experienced general opposition and been assaulted'... Collecting in Renvyle with six men sent by Mr. Blake - some armed...(we) were attacked by the people and pelted with stones' (21). There were also many requests for police protection for the collectors while carrying out their duties (22).

William E. Forster visited Renvyle in that same year (1847), to find the people on the verge of starvation. 'I now found their potatoes gone; what scanty crops they had gathered and eaten up together with the oats, including the seed corn; the turnips also consumed, nothing left but the cattle, and they quickly going; the sheep, the pigs, and even the poultry, almost all killed; eggs are hardly to be bought and I found on the Renvyle estate containing 850 families where almost every tenant owned a pig, there are now scarcely a dozen left' (23).

PLATE 3

Consequent to these and other reports, James and Mary Ellis, along with other members of the Religious Society of Friends, went to reside at Letterfrack in 1849. James Ellis, then aged 56, was retired, having led a very successful career in worsted manufacture in Leicester, England. James Ellis initially leased 959 acres from Francis Graham of Ballynakill and later purchased some 1,900 acres and proceeded to lay the foundations for the village as it is known today. The Ellises built a house (later to become a Christian Brothers Monastery), a meeting house/two storey schoolhouse (most recently used as a courthouse), a shop, a dispensary, a Temperance Hotel (Plate 3), and cottages for their workers. Their efforts at assisting the destitute and in developing the village and surrounding area were much commended. The Ellises are reputed, according to J. Forbes who visited in the Autumn of 1852, to have 'saved a whole population from utter ruin, nay from death itself. I was told by a gentleman on the spot, that but for the

Casson's Hotel, formerly The Temperance Hotel.
Courtesy of the National Library of Ireland.

constant employment and its accompaniment, constant and liberal pay, scores of the poor people in these secluded valleys must of necessity have sunk from mere starvation' during the famine (24).

Much can be learned of conditions at the time from letters written by Mary Ellis to her sisters Elizabeth Seebohm and Sarah Robson, while she resided in Letterfrack. The following account from a letter addressed to Sarah Robson, dated 30 April, 1849, vividly describes the harrowing circumstances families were reduced to during the famine in the Letterfrack area:

'Ann and I have been prowling this afternoon into such a cabin, about nine feet by six feet, with no furniture that I saw but a little stool about six inches high. This was immediately set for A., while I was pressed to sit down upon a little heap of litter-bedding. ... A happy looking woman at one end immediately reached down a bowl of cockles which she had been gathering off the strand and desired us to take some. ... She kept saying she had 'got no English,' at the same time making us understand very fairly their history, - that six years ago they had two cows and were doing well, when the famine came; one cow went after another, the last for £2 10s. Then her husband fell ill, and never since have they had food enough to eat. But the semi-nudity! The three poor little creatures had each a strip of woollen rag stitched upon them, but all in strips, not covering a limb or any side of their body, yet they were children one could love well. The eldest, five years old helped his father to an English word occasionally. They had lessened their cabin last week to sell two sticks for sixpence!' (25). (Plate 4).

The Ellises saw their role in the alleviation of the destitute primarily by means of affording regular employment (chiefly in agriculture), cash wages and in educating the population in methods which would 'have a direct bearing upon the permanent improvement of (their) condition ..., in promoting productive industry, and developing the resources of the country' (26). Due to the absence of resident landlords, and in many cases due to their financial situation, regular employment was difficult to secure and wages were low. In a letter to Elizabeth Seebohm, dated April 1849, Mary said that 'James finds there are complaints at his giving his labourers even eight pence a day ... his neighbours give only sixpence ... About thirty are at work, and more might be set to if our ship

PLATE 4

Typical house in Letterfrack in the nineteenth century.
Courtesy of the Illustrated London News Picture Library.

would bring us our barrows, &s' (27). In a letter in December of the same year, Mary again refers to James' progress in relation to providing employment. At this time he was employing some eighty men, mainly in the reclamation of land and planting of trees. Another letter from Mary to Elizabeth, dated December 1849, contains an account which clearly illustrates the poverty people were reduced to, and how a lack of basic clothing deterred people from leaving their hovels to avail of any assistance available: 'one poor man I found, a fortnight since, had been for months confined to his bed for want of a shirt to put on. So the gift of a few garments set him forth directly to the mountains to get willows for turf baskets, and he seems unwilling to take anything for them' (28).

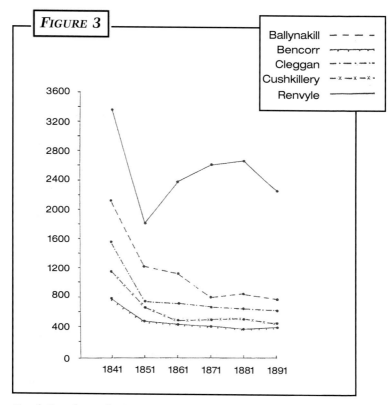

Population change by D.E.D. 1841 - 1891

The Ellises built a school house and employed a schoolmaster at their own expense. They hoped to cater for one hundred and twenty pupils. When Forbes visited Letterfrack in 1852, he reported that 'there were nearly sixty boys in the school and thirty two girls ... not one protestant...' (29). In 1855, Mary Ellis wrote to her sister Elizabeth that 'our school has just begun to mount up again, and got to between 40 and 50. A good many have come from Canon Wilberforce's school (of the Irish Church Mission Society), as they say the master is no good' (30). They also established a basket making industry which was revived by Sophia Sturge (an English Quaker) later in the century (31).

POPULATION 1841-1851

Change in population between 1841 and 1851 illustrates the devastating effect the famine had on the Irish population, though some may argue that these changes were inevitable notwithstanding the Great Famine. The population of the five D.E.Ds. comprising the study area in north west Galway was influenced by similar physical, social and economic factors, yet trends varied widely at both D.E.D. and townland levels. Between 1841 and 1851, the national population declined by 20% from 8.2 million to 6.5 million (32). Some one million of this loss has been attributed to the famine. In those years, Clifden Union lost 27% of its population through death, starvation and its associated illnesses, and outmigration. Sharp declines of 40% or more were experienced in the five D.E.D.s of Ballynakill, Bencorr, Cleggan, Cushkillary and Renvyle (Fig. 3). At townland level within each D.E.D., it is clear that variations occurred. The main pattern which emerged by 1851 was the concentration of population close to employment and relief centres (Fig. 4) (33).

Ballynakill D.E.D. extends south and east of Ballynakill Harbour and Barnaderg Bay. Of its population of 2,122 in 1841, 51% were settled in coastal townlands. In 1851 the total population had declined by 40% to 1,260. Between 1841 and 1851, marked declines took place in both coastal and inland townlands: Cloonederowen (-92%), Crocknaraw (-90%), Knocknahaw (-85%), Dooneen (-81%) and Ross (-85%). Townlands within closer proximity to Letterfrack village suffered lower losses, most likely due to the relief afforded by the Ellises in the form of food, clothing,

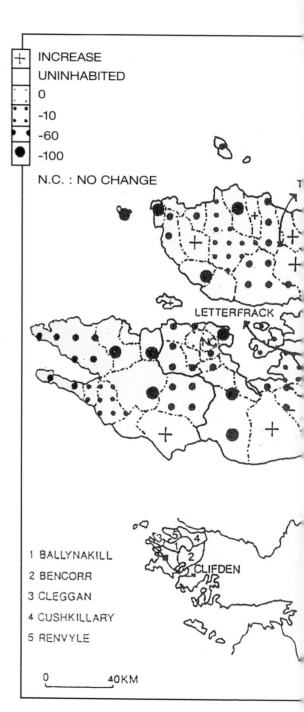

INCREASE

UNINHABITED

0

-10

-60

-100

N.C. : NO CHANGE

Population change (%) by townland 1841 - 1851

LETTERFRACK

N.C.

1 BALLYNAKILL

2 BENCORR

3 CLEGGAN

4 CUSHKILLARY

5 RENVYLE

CLIFDEN

0   40KM

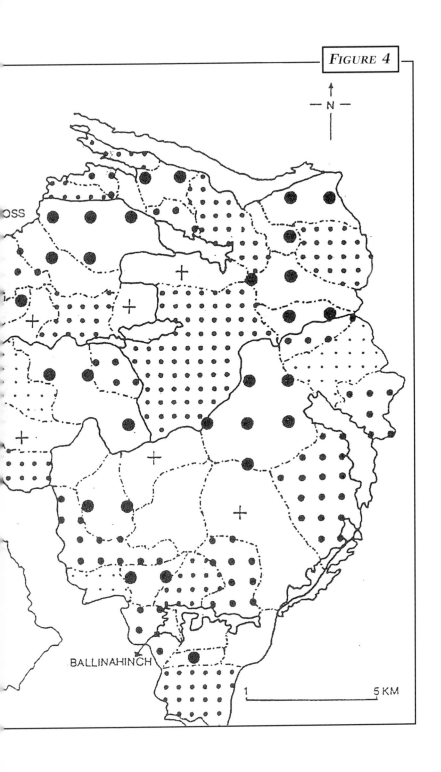

FIGURE 4

— N —

OSS

BALLINAHINCH

1   5 KM

education and most importantly, employment. The losses experienced were as low as 0.5% in Letterfrack, 20% in Baunogue and 24% in Rosleague. Population increased in three townlands in the environs of Letterfrack: Attirowerty (+10%), Keelkyle (+11%) and Moyard (+32%) (34).

Bencorr D.E.D. is situated in the south west of the Twelve Bens and has been sparsely populated throughout the years under review here. This D.E.D. has but one coastal townland, Derryadd West. Bencorr is however, traversed by streams, rivers and contains several lakes, many renowned for fishing. In 1841, 781 persons occupied Bencorr D.E.D. which is 25,679 acres in extent. Together, the coastal and lakeshore townlands contained 74% of the total population in 1841. In 1851, this figure had declined by 38%. As in Ballynakill D.E.D., population loss occurred in both inland and coastal townlands: Emlaghdaroe (-61%) Cloonbeg (-65%), Finnisglin (-54%) and Ballynafad (-51%). Tievebaun lost its total population in those years and slight increases occurred in Barnanang and Glencoaghan from 5 to 6 persons and 45 to 48 persons respectively (35).

Unlike Ballynakill D.E.D., landlords were absent in Bencorr during the famine. In 1848, the proprietor Thomas Martin died of fever contracted while visiting tenants and, in 1849, his daughter Mary was compelled to mortgage the estate to the London Law Life Assurance Company (36). Therefore an extensive but sparsely populated area was without a resident landlord to invest in development or to contribute to and organise relief schemes. Mr. Robertson, (the Company's agent) was reputed to have done much for the people by way of employment in the salmon and trout fisheries and in the preserving industry and also in land reclamation on his farm, all for which he paid regular wages (37).

Cleggan D.E.D. situated to the west of Ballynakill D.E.D. had the highest density of population of the five D.E.Ds. in 1841, with some 79% of the total population inhabiting the coastal townlands of Ballynew, Bundouglas, Cleggan and Knockbrack, situated in the north and west of the D.E.D. These townlands had the largest population numbers indicating perhaps a dependence on the sea. Declines as high as 90% and 84% were experienced in the townlands of Bundouglas and Sheeauns, respectively (38). The marked population decline in this D.E.D. (52% between 1841 and 1851) may be attributed to the absence of a resident landlord and to the fact that 'The 'gentry' who live in the neighbourhood seem to spend nothing hardly' (39) as Mary

Ellis observed in 1849. Cleggan D.E.D. was one of the most severely distressed areas in north west Galway. On Jan. 22 1847, W.E. Forster visited Cleggan and reported that 'the distress was appalling far beyond my power of description: I was quickly surrounded by a mob of men and women more like famished dogs than fellow-creatures' (40).

Cushkillary D.E.D. extends north from the northern boundaries of Bencorr D.E.D. to the southern shores of Killary Harbour, and west to the eastern boundaries of Renvyle and Ballynakill D.E.D.s. Between 1841 and 1851 the total population declined by 42% to 670. The population increased in the townlands of Lecknavarna and Salrock during this ten year period (41). This may be attributed to the assistance given by General Thompson of Salrock, by way of employment and food. In a letter dated January 1849, General Thompson stated that he had saved 500 people on his own estate from the relief list along with some of his neighbours' tenants (42). The population in Cushkillary was much reliant on the availability of work on pier and road construction organised as relief measures during the famine. In 1847, Forster commented on road building near Kylemore Lake where he 'found full a hundred men making a new road. After long cross-questioning, we learned that their wages did not average, taking one week with another, and allowing for broken days, more than four shillings and sixpence per week per head.... To get to their work many of the men have to walk five or even seven Irish miles. Four and six pence per week, thus earned, the sole source of a family of six; with Indian meal their cheapest food at 2s. 10d. to 4s. per stone ! What is this but slow death,- a mere enabling the patient to endure for a little longer time the disease of hunger?'(43)

Renvyle D.E.D., which is to the west of Cushkillary D.E.D., has an extensive coastline extending from Culfin to Renvyle Point to Barnaderg Bay. Its 13,571 acres were inhabited in 1841 by 3,367 persons, 95% of whom resided in coastal townlands. As in the other D.E.Ds., while the total population in Renvyle decreased by 46% between 1841 and 1851, variations occurred at townland level. It appears the population increased in townlands close to the villages of Letterfrack and Tullycross in those years: Cashleen (+29%), Currywongaun (+20%), Derryherbert (+18%) Gartnaglogh (+12%), Lemnaheltia (+14%) and Tullybeg (+88%) (44). The Blakes were the main landowners in this D.E.D. from 1680 to 1916. Forster, on his visit to the west in 1847, recorded that there was 'great distress in the neighbourhood of Renvyle ... several cases in which men had gone to the roads and worked for days without wages in the hope of obtaining (relief) tickets' (45) For those living in coastal townlands, especially in the Renvyle district, the main source of income was the kelp industry. J.M. Synge visited the west at this time and met an old man who told him that 'they are letting me out advanced meal and flour from the ship...and I'm to pay it back when I burn a ton of kelp in the summer' (46).

OVERVIEW

Living conditions did not improve immediately the famine was over, owing to the slow progress of favourable changes. In Clifden Union in 1850, some 20,343 were in receipt of some form of relief and, by 1851, this number had declined to 7,190 persons (47). Forbes reported that, at the time of his visit, there were some 840 inmates in Clifden workhouse. 'In June 1851, they had 3,600 persons on their books and he is sure that among these there were not more than 30 or 40 protestants' (48).

It is clear that employment and regular cash wages were most important to the population of these D.E.Ds. throughout the famine period. Though four of the D.E.Ds. possess an extensive shoreline along with many lakes and rivers, the fishing industry for the most part was not a viable enterprise. 'In some few villages there is a little fishing but it is so slight and partial an extent that it can hardly be looked upon as a resource' (49). The industry's lack of development was in part due to a lack of suitable piers and harbours. Many of the district's piers were but in their initial stages of development during the famine. Work was carried out as part of the Government's relief works when funds were available for this purpose, resulting in the completion of works being a slow process. At Ballynakill Harbour in 1849, the Society of Friends established a fishing station but its operation ceased two years later. They had supplied 'a fleet made up of ten curraghs and other boats fully equipped with nets, lines and all gear was provided at a cost of £300' (50). For those living in coastal townlands, especially in the Renvyle district, the main source of income derived from the sea was in the kelp industry.

The vast majority of the population of north west Galway were dependent on small holdings, which many lost through eviction or desertion during the famine. The people were very much at the mercy of the landlords and highly dependent on them for employment and financial aid. 'The poor peasants struggle to live on scanty crops which these steep hillsides will yield: whilst they have neither capital nor knowledge nor encouragement to drain and improve their existing state' (51). At this time the work of the Religious Society of Friends proved invaluable to the inhabitants of the townlands in the environs of Letterfrack.

Those living within easy reach of assistance were clearly more comfortable as H. Coulter, on his visit to the area in 1862, observed that 'shortly after leaving Clifden the miserable hovels became fewer and fewer, until they completely disappear; and the same observation is applicable to the district lying between Letterfrack and Leenane' (52). In 1892, it was also recorded that 'as compared to other Congested Districts, Letterfrack is well circumstanced for the employment of agricultural labourers, but there are two portions of the district where labour is required by the people–Renvyle and Baunoges' (53).

REFERENCES

1   S.H. Cousens, 'The Regional Variation in Mortality During the Great Irish Famine', *P. R. I. A.* Vol 63 Section C, (1963), p. 127-140.
2   D.B. Grigg, *Population and Agrarian Change A Historical Perspective* (Cambridge 1980), p. 116.
3   Devon Commission Vol. ll (1845), evidence no.499, p. 478.
4   Ibid., evidence no. 494, p. 474.
5   Ibid., evidence no. 493, p. 491.
6   Ibid., evidence no. 494, p. 472.
7   Ibid., evidence no. 491, p. 466.
8   Ibid., evidence no. 491, p.467.
9   Ibid., evidence no. 499, p. 478.
10 Ibid., evidence no. 499, p. 478.
11 John O'Connor, *The Workhouses of Ireland The Fate of Ireland's Poor* (Dublin 1995).
12 Ibid., p.81.
13 Ibid.
14 Ibid.
15 Ibid.
16 W. E. Forster, *Religious Society of Friends Distress in Ireland Committee Minute Book* (London 1847), p. 2.
17 O'Connor, op. cit.
18 J.H. Ashworth, *The Saxon in Ireland or the Rambles of an Englishman in Search of Settlement in the West of Ireland* (London 1851).
19 J. Hack Tuke, *A Visit to Connaught in the Autumn of 1847* (1848), P.7.
20 Ibid., p.14.
21 National Archives *Outrage Reports Letter from a rate collector Clifden Union to J. A. Dopping* dated Oct.4 1847, mss.11/863.
22 Ibid.,
23 Forster, op cit., p.155-156.
24 J. Forbes, *A Sketchbook of Travel in Ireland Vol 1* (London 1853) p.261
25 B. & E. Seebohm (Edited by their sons), *The Private Memoirs of B. & E. Seebohm,* (London 1873), p.361-362.
26 Religious Society of Friends, *Distress in Ireland Committee Minute Book* (London 1847), p.2.
27 Seebohm, op.cit., p.359.
28 Ibid., p. 366.
29 J. Forbes, op. cit., p.261.
30 Seebohm, op. cit., p. 390.
31 W.R. Hughes, *Sophia Sturge A Memoir* (London 1940)
32 Census of Population 1841-1851
33 Eibhlín NÍ Scannláin, "Athrú Tírdhreacha i bPáirc Náisiúnta Chonamara agus an Cheantair Máguaird ó Thús an Naoú Céad Déag", 1988. (Unpublished).

34 Ibid.
35 Ibid.
36 M. Edgeworth, *Tour in Connemara and the Martins of Ballynahinch* (London 1950)
37 G. Preston White, *A Tour in Connemara with remarks on its great Physical Capabilities* (London 1849): Forbes, op. cit.
38 Ní Scannláin, op. cit.
39 Seebohm, op.cit., p. 362.
40 Forster, op cit., p. 132.
41 Ní Scannláin, op.cit.
42 *Hodgkin Correspondence* (1849) Box 1 Folder 3, Religious Society of Friends Library Dublin.
43 Forster, op. cit., p. 154.
44 Ní Scannláin, op.cit.
45 Forster, op. cit., p. 269.
46 *J.M. Synge, In Wicklow, West Kerry and Connemara* (London 1919), p. 186.
47 Ní Scannláin, op.cit.
48 Forbes, op.cit., p.249.
49 Forster, op. cit., p.155.
50 C. Woodham Smith, *The Great Hunger* (London 1981 reprint), p. 289.
51 W. Foster,*The People of Ireland* (London 1846), p. 269.
52 H. Coulter, *The West of Ireland* (London 1862), p. 125.
53 *Baseline Reports to The Congested Districts Board Part ll* (1892), p. 6.

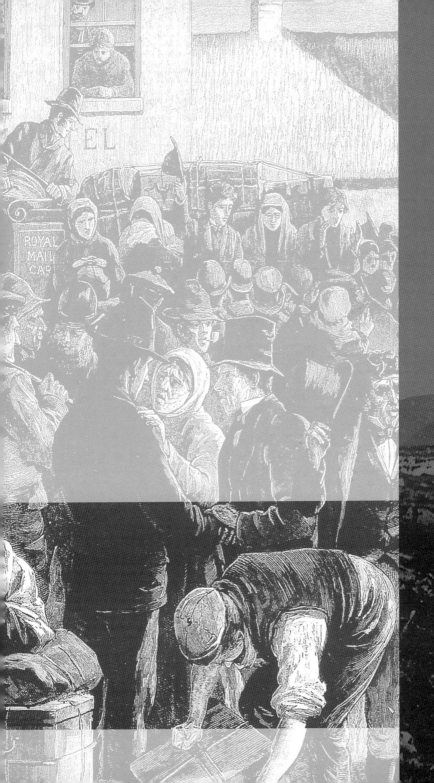

CONTEXT

The post-famine period WAS highly influential in moulding perhaps one of the most important periods in Irish rural life. The famine, evictions and general economic climate convinced tenants of the insecurity of their position and many were determined that they would not be in that position in the future. Owing to continuing evictions, the poor harvests of 1877-79, and tenant distress and dissatisfaction in general, the Irish National Land League was founded in 1879, under the leadership of Charles Stewart Parnell and Michael Davitt (1). Its main objective was to reduce rents which had increased by 12.5% between 1865 and 1880, due to rising livestock prices between 1850 and the mid 1870s and subsequent competition for grazing land, and to convince the Government that tenant proprietorship of their holdings was the only solution to the multitude of problems prevailing in rural Ireland at the time (2). Several Land Acts were introduced between 1881 and 1903 encouraging the transfer of land proprietorship from the landlords to their former tenants. This resulted in a steady increase in farm ownership and in the number of medium size holdings. These changes proved most favourable to livestock production leading to increases in the number of cattle and sheep on farms.

The process of land transfer in particular provoked considerable hostility between small farmers and graziers or ranch style farmers. A typical farm in the area of north west Galway in the early 1860s according to the Saunders News Letter correspondent Henry Coulter, consisted of 'five or even less to twelve and fifteen acres and the rents are high. Each farmer had a cow or two, a pig and a couple of sheep or more, according to the size of his holding' (3). Livestock production became well established in Clifden Union during the second half of the nineteenth century due to the continuous increase in the number of medium size holdings and improved livestock prices (4). The farmers found that livestock production made 'their lives easier and less laborious and 'they find also that the land pays better in grass than in tillage' (5). The most notable sources of employment in north west Galway during this period included basket making and road and railway construction. The introduction of the Bianconi cars and the opening of the Galway to Clifden Railway line in 1895 encouraged tourism in the area and also the commercial development of Clifden town. These developments also made Irish ports and cities more accessible to the population, in particular those looking to improve their lot by migration or emigration. The pattern of population decline established in 1851 continued throughout the latter half of the nineteenth century.

Towards the end of the nineteenth century, a large proportion of the inhabitants of Iar Connacht were still living on a subsistence basis as in the pre famine period. 'The principal means possessed by the people of this district are: Farming including mountain grazing; Employment as agricultural labourers; Kelp-making; Sea fishing' (6). Major changes occurred in the numbers of holdings, size of holdings, land ownership and the agricultural economy in the post-famine period. These changes had been initiated in the pre-famine era but the famine played a more decisive role in their imposition throughout Ireland. D.A. Grigg found that the move towards pastoralism in Irish agriculture had begun following the Napoleonic wars and the period of low cereal prices which ensued (7).

LAND ACQUISITION

During the post-famine period, many landlords were faced with financial difficulties and, in 1849, the Encumbered Estates Court was established under which many estates were mortgaged or sold and subdivided. In north west Galway such estates included the Martin estate at Ballynahinch, and the D'Arcy of Clifden estate which went on sale in 1852 and included the townland of Kylemore (Plate 5). The Blakes of Renvyle were forced to lease lands between Tooreena and Lettergesh to Canon Wilberforce who in turn sublet to St. John L. Clowes (8). During this period, the acquisition of large pasture holdings by graziers was commonplace. This was facilitated by the availability of untenanted arable and pasture land due to evictions or the financial problems which compelled landlords to sell their property.

In 1870, the first Landlord Tenant Act was passed by the British Parliament (the first time tenant rights were recognised). Under this Act, tenants were entitled to compensation for any improvements made to their holdings should they face eviction (9). However incidents such as that in Ballynakill Parish where a member of the

PLATE 5

Clifden Castle.
Courtesy of the National Library of Ireland.

Gannon family, who was evicted by Mr. Graham (in order to convert the holding into grazing land), applied for redress and did not receive compensation, discouraged others and this was the last such case in the area (10). In 1870, only 3% of Irish holdings were owner occupied and by 1908, this had increased to 46% (11). Overall, the 1870 Act achieved little and in 1881, Gladstone's Land Act was passed under which the 'three Fs' were granted to the whole of Ireland (fair rent, fixity of tenure and free sale). The Irish Land Commission was established under this Act and was authorised by the state to advance capital to tenants to facilitate the purchase of their holdings (12). This Land Act was seen as the best way to resolve the agitation experienced during the 1870s and was followed by the Ashbourne Act of 1885 and the Wyndham Act of 1903. The change of land ownership from landlord to tenant during the late nineteenth century was mainly brought about by the reallocation of land and resettlement by both the Irish Land Commission and the C.D.B. established in 1891 (13).

As the Irish National Land League gained the support of tenants, and in some cases landlords, branches were formed in many areas. The Clifden branch of the Land League had its first meeting in Clifden on September 10, 1879 and in 1880 a Letterfrack branch was founded (14). After some time the organization resorted to boycotting and violence, and landlords, such as Mitchell Henry at Kylemore, then withdrew their support. In the area of north west Galway incidents included the murder of Mr. Graham's herder, his son and the sergeant who was investigating the case (15). Rents were boycotted on the Henry estate and on the Blake estate. During the late 1870s, Mrs. Caroline Blake was managing the Renvyle estate and due to the no-rents manifesto was compelled to accommodate paying guests. In 1883, Renvyle House became Renvyle Hotel. During the non-payment of rents period, guests included Edith Oenone Sommerville and Violet Martin Ross who noted that the tenants regularly drove livestock on to Mrs. Blake's property and she had to go 'out day after day to drive off her land the trespassing cattle, sheep and horses that were as regularly driven on it again as soon as her back was turned' (16).

The transfer of land proprietorship from landlords to the former tenants was primarily concluded between 1891 and 1923, with the aid of various Land Purchase Parliamentary Acts such as Wyndham's Land Act 1903, Birrell's Act 1909, and the Land Act of 1923. As with previous land legislation, the 1903 Act had but limited success: 'In Connemara at least the landlords' exorbitant and prohibitive demands have rendered the Land Act of 1903 inoperative and have made land purchase impossible' (17). Estates and extensive untenanted tracts of land were purchased by both the C.D.B. and the Estates Commissioners and eventually, under the Land Act of 1923, the 'principle of compulsion to expedite land transfer' was accepted (18). The various land qualities were divided among farmers in any one area by way of 'striping' (enclosed, regular, usually rectangular shaped strips of land) giving rise to a ladder-like field system characteristic of the contemporary landscape as seen on the 6" O.S. maps (19). Occasionally, the landlords striped the land when consolidating holdings, as did the Blakes of Renvyle (20). The occupation of pasture lands by graziers infuriated the small farmers and led to a feud similar to that experienced between the landlords and tenants some decades previously and involved similar intimidation tactics. In 1889 the average valuation per head of population in each District Electoral Division illustrates that the average for the D.E.Ds. of Renvyle, Cushkillary and Cleggan was 13s.4d.; Ballynakill £1.6s.8d. - £2.0.0. and Bencorr £2.0.0. - £2.13s. 4d. (21). At this time the national average was £2.13s.4d. The enmity between graziers and small farmers was further exacerbated by the 1903 Land Act and continued until 1909. In Clifden Union this enmity was due to the fact that there were some '3,000 families living on the bogs and marshes with a valuation under £4 while on the other hand you have 88 non resident graziers holding between them 68,000 acres of the best land in the district,' during the early twentieth century (22).

In evidence to the Commissioners of the C.D.B., many expressed concern about the fate of the small farmers of Iar Connacht should existing circumstances persist. Among the expanses of land the C.D.B. was interested in acquiring for subdivision was part of the Thompson property in Cushkillary D.E.D. This comprised 'about 8,000 acres of which 1,400 consists of untenanted arable pasture and about 2,000 acres more are easily reclaimable and suitable for agricultural holdings' (23). The C.D.B. also attempted to purchase the Prior property (Ross House) on which holdings ranged from 15s. to £2 in valuation, but Mrs. Armstrong Lushington-Tulloch of Shamboolard Hall succeeded in securing the property: 'There was one property there that in old times had about 70 tenants and there are not two on it now' (24). Among the lands purchased by the C.D.B. in north west Co. Galway between 1891 and 1923, were parts of the Thompson, Blake, Tulloch and Lord Ardilaun estates (25).

Not all agreed that it was best to enlarge existing small holdings. A witness from the Renvyle area expressed the view that 'the small holders get on very well but suppose they want more land. I don't think they have any reason to get mine' (26). Another opinion was that the 'outcry about uneconomic holdings in the west is largely due to the fact that the land is held by tenants who will work no more than they can help and appear to have no ambition to improve their circumstances' (27).

LAND IMPROVEMENT

In the post-famine period, extensive land improvement schemes continued and, by the mid 1870s, the total area of improved land in Ireland reached its peak at 12,972,997 acres but declined following the depression of 1877-79 (28). The tenants had few rights to their holdings and due to the insecurity involved they had little interest or incentive to improve their lot. The tenants attitude, as Coulter recorded from an old man in Connemara in 1862, was 'ah, why should I trouble myself about it? Sure wouldn't the rent be raised on me or how do I know that I'd be there tomorrow?' (29). Few improvements were carried out on large properties where landlords were non-resident such as on the Ballynahinch Estate. Coulter visited this estate to find the land in 'exactly the same state as when it came into their hands' (The London Law Life Assurance Company) 'undrained, unfenced, unimproved in any respect' (30).

Land reclamation was in the main carried out by those landlords interested in developing their property. Among those improving landlords in Iar Connacht was James Ellis of Letterfrack. The Rev J. D. Smith revisited the district in 1853, and remarked that 'Letterfrack a few years ago was a barren rock; it is now a crown of beauty .... It is indeed a gem, speaking with sufficient modesty in the midst of surrounding rock; an oasis crowning the bold and magnificent mountain wild with the most striking effect of contrast and variety, altogether 'won' by money and skill from nature's uncultivated waste' (31). Other favourable commentators were Forbes 1852, Townsend 1853 and Rev. McManus 1863. Reclamation was also underway on the

Eastwood estate at Addergoole by 1851. 'Mr. Eastwood seems to have set to work in good earnest, having built himself an excellent house, ... and secured an estate beautifully situated in the gorge of the vale ... in all directions the work of reclamation was going on' (32). The Eastwoods settled here in 1847 and the property was offered for sale under the courts in 1862. During the famine years, the Eastwoods experienced considerable antagonism. Thomas Eastwood's eldest son was on the list of candidates for the office of Poor Law Guardian along with Mr. Blake of Renvyle and Mr. Dancer of Letterfrack in 1849. All three were denounced from the altar by the Rev. W. Flannelly of Ballynakill who declared that 'Mr. Blake is the best of the three but bad is the best' (33).

The Eastwoods and their servants (many of whom were English) were the victims of intimidation tactics for weeks to follow. One incident occurred not far from Letterfrack when some of the servants were returning from Clifden with stores when they were met by a group who told them that 'if they the servants, did not leave the country, they would murder them as well as their masters' (34). This property was purchased by Mitchell Henry circa 1864, along with lands purchased from the Blakes of Renvyle. Mitchell Henry (who built Kylemore Castle) was probably the most renowned reclaimer of wasteland in this district during the second half of the nineteenth century. On his visit to the west of Ireland in 1884, A. I. Shand wrote 'When he (Mitchell Henry) came to Kylemore some twenty years ago, the land was nothing but undrained bog with the exception of one little patch of reclamation where Mr. Eastwood, an Englishman, had settled after the famine, Mr. Henry has turned no less than 3,000 bad acres into rich grazing and productive arable land' (35). The tenants continued to reclaim small patches mainly by cultivating crops in ridges and by fertilizing with seaweed, coral sand or lime. On the Henry estate the tenants benefited both from the example given and 'they get what lime they want from sundry kilns on the property and their crops on land borrowed from the bogs are at least as good as their landlords' (36). Mitchell Henry's Estate was sold to the Benedictine Nuns in 1918 where they established a girls' boarding school.

FARMING IN POST-FAMINE IAR CONNACHT

The importance of grassland in Irish farming, especially in the west, is formed by those factors which deter tillage. Agriculturally, Ireland may be divided in two: east and west of the Shannon. The west is dominated by mountainous areas and poor quality soils which hinder cropping, while to the east relief and climatic conditions are more conducive to arable farming. A similar division between east and west exists in County Galway with Lough Corrib as the dividing line. The eastern part of the county mainly contains well drained limestone based soils, traditionally grazier country, while mountainous granite, schists and quartzite-based land in the west has for long been the home of subsistence farms and a mixed agricultural economy. During the years 1850-1900, the divisions between the east and the west of Ireland became further entrenched. 'The number of cattle on Irish farms increased by over 60%, and the number of sheep more than doubled. The tillage declined from 4.3 million to 2.4 million acres and the rural population from 5.3 million to 3.0 million' (37). It became obvious that medium size holdings were best suited to support livestock production. Such holdings generally ranged from 15-50 acres in size. The number of medium-size holdings increased gradually as large holdings were divided and smaller holdings were consolidated.

In Clifden Union in 1851, there was a total of 2,412 holdings and by 1860 the number had increased by 62%. During this period marked increases occurred in the 15-30 acres (370-725), 30-50 acres (58-232) and 50-100acres (64-156) categories. The number of holdings in the 5-15 acres group increased by 58% between 1851 and 1860, and accounted for approximately 40% of total holdings in both years. The total number of holdings in the Union decreased by 5% between 1860 and 1880, probably due to the crop failures of 1877-1879 and the widespread emigration which followed. The most significant increases in numbers between 1880 and 1890 occurred in the 15-30(7.5%), 30-50(19%), and 50-100(5%) acres categories (38).

As the second half of the nineteenth century progressed, it became clear that there was considerable competition between pasture and tillage acreage on holdings. In 1851, Ireland's highest tillage acreage was recorded, but it gradually declined (39). Between 1851 and 1860, the area under tillage in Clifden Union increased by 59% to 10,622 acres and was followed by continuous decline. In 1890, tillage accounted for 7,674 acres while pasture had increased to 182,013 acres (94% of the total area) (40). As the number of medium-size holdings and the area under pasture in Clifden Union increased, so too did the number of livestock. Cattle increased in number by 67% between 1851 and 1860 and by 33% between 1880 and 1890 to 18,093. Sheep farming has been an essential enterprise in north west Galway. Between 1851 and 1860, the total number of sheep in Clifden Union increased by 133% and in 1890 had reached 43,768 (an increase of 318% on 1851) (41).

During the second half of the nineteenth century, Iar Connacht became an area of mixed agricultural economy primarily in beef cattle and lamb production. The small farmer in north west Galway became the livestock breeder and supplied the store graziers of Connaught and Leinster.

PLATE 6

Emigration scene in Clifden.
Courtesy of the Illustrated London News Picture Library.

This system was documented in the C.D.B. Reports of 1907 as follows: '(1) the small farmer breeds the stock; (2) the store-grazier of Connaught buys the young stock from the small farmers; (3) the store-grazier, after a year or a year and a half passes them on to the Leinster graziers who finish them' (42). Livestock production became further entrenched in Iar Connacht. during the latter half of the nineteenth and early twentieth century. The number of medium size holdings, which are best suited to livestock production in the west, continued to increase in Clifden Union and, by 1917, represented 71% of the total holdings (43).

POPULATION CHANGE 1851-1891

Between 1851 and 1891, despite some increases in population experienced in individual townlands, the overall pattern at D.E.D. level was one of decline (Fig. 3). In 1877-1879, famine conditions resumed over much of the country due to bad weather conditions. Widespread emigration followed the famine of 1877-79, chiefly from the west. According to D. Fitzpatrick, during 'the early 1880s, 10,000 impoverished westerners were removed under the supervision of the Quaker banker, James Hack Tuke, funding being shared between the state and 'Mr. Tuke's Committee' under which some 2,000 people were assisted to emigrate from Clifden Union between 1882 and 1884' (44) (Plate 6).

In Ballynakill D.E.D., the first increase in population in the post-famine period took place between 1871 and 1881 (from 801 to 860 persons) but by 1891 a decline of 10% had occurred. In 1891, as in 1851, the population was concentrated in areas of employment opportunities and better farmland. For instance, the inhabitants of the townlands of Letterfrack, Moyard, Attirowerty and Addergoole accounted for 38%, 12%, 10% and 6% of the total population of the D.E.D. respectively. The Ellises were compelled to return to England in 1857 due to James' ill-health. Mary Ellis died in August of that year and James was deceased in 1867. Their Estate was purchased by John Charles Hall and later became the property of the Archbishop of Tuam. Letterfrack Industrial School was established on this property in 1887.

In Bencorr D.E.D., increases in population took place in the townlands of Glencoaghan, Derrynaglaun, Ballynafad

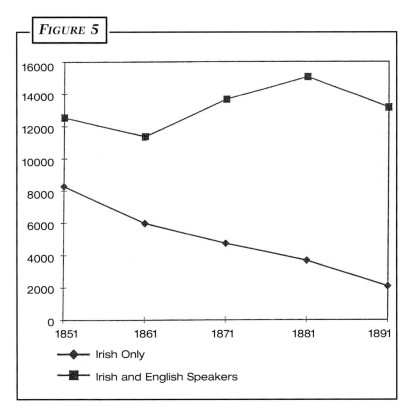

FIGURE 5

The status of the Irish Language in the Barony of Ballynahinch 1851 - 1891.

and Tievebaun, between 1851 and 1891, and indicate movement of people from less accessible and mountainous parts of the D.E.D. towards newly-developed roads. The development of communications afforded employment during construction and provided easy access to towns and villages.

The decreases in population in Cleggan D.E.D. between 1841 and 1851, initiated a continuous trend of decline. A large percentage of the population remained settled in the western portion of the D.E.D. in 1891 as in 1851 (Ballynew, Cloon and Knockbrack accounted for 18%, 12% and 31% of the total population respectively). Though the population increased in Cushkillary D.E.D. between 1861 and 1881, a decline of 9% occurred over the years 1881-1891. The townlands of Salrock, Glassilaun, Culfin and Kylemore were inhabited by a large proportion of the total population of the D.E.D. in 1891. The increase in population in Culfin in 1891 was attributed to subdivision of land. The concentration of population in the other townlands indicates the influential role of employment on population levels.

The population of Renvyle D.E.D. began an upward trend following the famine and, by 1881, it had increased by 46% on the 1851 figure. This was due to the reallocation of lands and resettlement which took place during these years. This period of increase was followed by a fall of 15% between 1881 and 1891. As in other D.E.Ds., the population was concentrated in townlands affording employment opportunities such as Currywongaun and Pollacappul in which Kylemore Castle is situated (45).

It is interesting to note the pattern of steady decline in the use of the Irish language that accompanied the overall decline in population during this period 1851-1891 (statistics available at Barony level only). The numbers of people in the Barony of Ballynahinch who spoke only Irish show a pattern of steady decline even when the overall population of the Barony experienced brief periods of increase in 1871 and 1881. While those who spoke only Irish represented 34.56% of the Barony's population in 1851, this proportion fell to 10.06% in 1891 (Fig 5). The decline of the Irish language in this area may be attributed to various factors: the establishment of Clifden as the area's main commercial centre; the high rate of emigration from Irish speaking areas resulting in those who were left being less interested in safeguarding the language; the education system of the time which did not recognise the Irish language. While many of those who visited and assisted the population during and after the Famine did much for development of the area, the message to the local population again would have been that they too would be comfortably well off if they had some command of the English language.

COMMUNICATIONS

As in the pre-famine period, it was necessary to supplement agricultural income with fishing, kelp-making, illicit distillation, knitting and weaving. Other employment sources included road and railway construction, organised as relief works, and the basket industry at Letterfrack. At the beginning of the twentieth century yet another appeal was made to the Government via the C.D.B. for financial support on behalf of the inhabitants of Iar Connacht. 'Once again on behalf of Clifden and Connemara, that so long as our piers are left unmade, our quarries left unworked, our fisheries undeveloped and our large grazing tracts untenanted, so long on the part of the Government will opportunities be missed, duties neglected and promises unfulfilled' (46). Relief works were operated by the Government and local bodies to improve communications throughout Connemara in the hope that economically viable industries and businesses would be established and developed and that living conditions in general would be improved.

The inadequacy of roads in some parts of north west Galway hindered the development of local amenities. For instance a marble quarry owned by Francis Graham 'was let on lease to a Belfast firm, but the difficulty of removing the marble owing to the want of a road leading to Letterfrack was so great that the lease was surrendered to the owner' (47). Among the Relief works in operation during the distress of 1890-91, as illustrated on an 1891 Relief map, was the Tully road from Letterfrack to Renvyle, the Baunogues Road, and repairs being carried out on Derryinver Pier and road (commenced May 4, 1891) (48). Some of these roads however remained unfinished into the early twentieth century. For example, it was reported in evidence to the C.D.B. in 1907 that the road 'which runs towards Loughnahillion... (was) a most important road to join north and south Connemara...at present there is a gap in the centre... about a mile and a half...we extended it by relief works during the last dozen years by two miles' (1893-1907). A mile and a half of this road remained unfinished due to a lack of capital as this particular piece of road was not within C.D.B. jurisdiction (49).

The most celebrated form of public transport to travel Connemara roads during the nineteenth century was the Bianconi horse-car (later replaced by the Long car/mail car) (Plate 7). Italian born Carlo Bianconi arrived in Ireland in 1802 and engaged in print selling. His extensive experience of travelling on Irish roads 'opened his eye to the possibilities of a cheap transport system' and in 1815 the first scheduled car service between Clonmel and Cahir commenced (50). By 1845 the Bianconi car service had extended nationwide including a service between Galway City and Clifden. From 1851 on, the Galway to Clifden run operated a feeder service to the Dublin to Galway railway.

PLATE 7

Mailcar on Letterfrack – Clifden Road.
Courtesy of the National Library of Ireland.

The Bianconi cars introduced tourists to Connemara and provided organised tours. In 1867, Bianconi retired and the Galway to Clifden branch was purchased by his agent Mr. K. O'Brien of Eyre Square, Galway. Mr. O'Brien maintained the service until the Galway to Clifden railway line was opened in 1895 after which tours continued to be operated throughout Connemara; from Clifden to Westport via Letterfrack, for instance (51). In 1895 W.B.Hartland travelled this route and on the subject of roads in the vicinity of Letterfrack said, 'The roads are well kept, with gravel and sand from 'allotted pits' in the district; no stones used; good for the poor horses' (52).

The Galway to Clifden Railway line (Fig. 1) was mooted under the Light Railways (Ireland) Act in 1889 (53). This line was first proposed in the 1860s, but the planned route was disputed. In 1885 the Allport Commission accepted the Galway route via Moycullen, Ross, Oughterard, Maam Cross and Ballynahinch, as opposed to the south Connemara route, which rendered the accepted 'railway line practically useless to the great bulk of the population of Connemara living on the seaboard between Galway and Roundstone' (54). When the Light Railway Act of 1889 was passed, Mr. Balfour was chief Secretary for Ireland 'and being anxious to improve the condition of the country and the people for which object the special Act was passed, pressed the Midland and Great Western Railway Company (M.G.W.R.C.) to commence work as relief works, a request which was generously responded to by the chairman and directors' (55). Wages for railway construction were far superior to those in agriculture: 'wages on the railway (were) 14s. per week; farmers wages (were) 8s. to 9s' (56).

The line was 48 miles and 550 feet in length and commenced ' by a junction with the Midland Great Western Railway of Ireland system at Galway station' (57). The route was described as follows by J.H. Ryan: 'The line passes through the eastern outskirts of the town and under Prospect Hill by a tunnel, the only one on the railway... The line thence proceeds over the Corrib River by a bridge, an imposing and elegant structure of steel. Crossing the bridge, the line traverses for miles the west side of the River Corrib, passing deserted mansions, breweries and factories. On the east side of the river is seen Terryland.... the ruined castellated mansion of the De Burgos; and next Menlo Castle, the picturesque residence of Sir Valentine Blake Bart;... The railway thence traverses the west shore of

Lough Corrib. ... on the left or western side of the line are seen the range of hills that stretch from Galway to Oughterard. Along their slopes are the well-wooded demesnes of Woodstock, Danesfield, Drimcong, Ross, Killaguile etc., with ruins of mansion, castle and abbey, and also the village of Moycullen...where there is a station of that name beyond which, and along the line are seen the picturesque woods, glades and lakes about Drimcong, and Ross; at the latter is the station of that name'.

'As the town of Oughterard is approached, the district presents a more civilized aspect. Leaving Maam Cross station, the line now enters the Joyce Country and Connemara proper, ... the line passes Lough Shindilla, Lough Oorid and through the valley of the Recess River to Recess Station, at 35.5 miles, on Glendalough Lake. Leaving Recess, the line passes the southern shores of Derryclare Lake, Athry Lough and the east end of Ballynahinch Lake, thence by Lough Nabrucka, Ballinafad Lough and Killeen Lake' to Clifden Station (58).

The line was constructed in three sections. Section 1, Galway to Oughterard, opened January 1st 1895: Sections 2 and 3, Oughterard to Clifden, opened July 1st 1895. A grant of £264,000 was allocated by the Government to the M.G.W.R.C. for the construction of the line 'on the condition that it should be maintained and worked by them' (59). The extra expenses of £181,000 were met by the M.G.W.R.C. Along the line were built seven stations, eighteen gate keepers' houses at public road crossings, twenty eight bridges and thirteen accommodation bridges (60). The Galway to Clifden line was especially popular with tourists and in 1903 the M.G.W.R.C. introduced a special service, 'a 'tourist express' from Dublin to Galway and it continued non stop to Clifden' (61). On April 20th 1935, the line was closed when 'the company declared the line an uneconomic unit of their service and a heavy drain on their resources' (62).

LOCAL EMPLOYMENT OPPORTUNITIES

A basket-making industry was first established by James and Mary Ellis in Letterfrack during the famine. In 1888, it was re-established by an English Quaker named Sophia Sturge. She first visited Ireland in September 1887, and became aware of the distress of the poor. Sophia Sturge returned in Autumn 1888 and settled at Letterfrack, having spent the previous year travelling and gaining knowledge of basket-making and willow-farming in England. She also travelled to the famous basket making village of Origny-en-Thièrach in France, to further her knowledge of the industry and to perfect her skills. In Origny she purchased the various blocks and tools necessary to establish the industry at Letterfrack (63).

Lessons in basket-making commenced in September 1888 with one pupil, in the local court house. Once the winter months had elapsed 'she started teaching a group of boys in the evenings after school time' and a girls' class 'sprang up almost of itself and started to learn chip-plaiting and bonnet-making' (64). The industry expanded and after two years the court house was unable to accommodate pupils, supervisors and equipment. At this time those employed were earning 'Wages.... higher than any in the Connemara district' and as the industry prospered the hope was expressed that 'this desolate and poor district will be transformed into a thriving and industrious locality' (65).

With the financial assistance of George Tangye of Birmingham, Sophia Sturge purchased 'a piece of land four acres in extent.. for the sum of twenty pounds, and on January 6th, 1891, Sophia received a clod of earth from the former occupier, Michael Joyce, as the customary symbol of the transfer of tenant rights' (66). By September 1st 1891, the building of a house and factory was completed at the site which had been 'formally christened 'Shancoleir' by Sophia's English and Irish friends (67) (Plate 8).

The variety of baskets produced in the factory was described by Sophia's friend Alexandrina Peckover who visited the industry in 1889. 'The baskets that the boys make are of different sizes, the largest being about a foot and a quarter long and eight inches deep. The smallest are about quarter the size..... The largest size is 3s. or 3s. 6d., and when filled with moss and primroses 1s. extra is charged for it. The smallest size is 1s. or 1. 6d. and sixpence extra is charged for the filling' (68). The girls who attended in the evenings made 'fancy baskets' of Norwegian chip and of palm leaves from the West Indies. (In all sixty five various items of wicker-work were made.) 'Besides baskets and hampers of all sorts were chairs, dog baskets, drawing room kennels, tea-tables, hand carts, writing desks, cupboards, stools, bookstands and dolls' furniture' (69).

During its first year, the enterprise made and sold a thousand baskets and in its second year of operation, over

£250 was received for items manufactured and the industry gained a clientele of 1,000 'inspite of a journey of over fifty miles to the nearest railway station the baskets were going out by hundreds' (70). Sophia also introduced a basket-making teacher named Camille to Letterfrack during the second year. He was from Origny and spent a year in Letterfrack providing instruction in the finer types of basketry (71).

It was necessary to import the osiers from Norway, Birmingham and Somersetshire. This proved an expensive practice: 'prices paid for peeled osiers range from 2d. to 5d. per 1b. according to quality and from extremely fine quality they are even sold as high as 9d. per 1b' (72). Sophia commenced willow-farming in Letterfrack on wet hillside land acquired from the Christian Brothers at the Industrial School and from Mitchell Henry of Kylemore Castle (73). A boiler was installed at Shancoleir in 1892, and instructions on the preparation of willow rods for the industry were provided by a Southport basket-maker. The osiers grown at Shancolier did not suffice the industry and osiers continued to be imported (74).

Sophia Sturge spent seven years developing the enterprise and, in 1896, was compelled to return to England due to ill health and her mother's death. Management was then secured by the C.D.B. who appointed a Birmingham basket-maker as supervisor. In 1879, W.J.D. Walker inspected the industry for the C.D.B. to establish the profitability of continuing to subsidise the industry. According to Walker's report, the employment afforded by the industry was of the greatest value to the neighbourhood. Those employed 'As a rule they reside at a considerable distance, those visited living some four or five miles off on a bare and rocky mountain slope west of Letterfrack in the E.D. of Renvyle. In the Basket factory I saw twelve boys at work, their earnings ranged from 4s. to 13s. per week. Seven of the older lads who have been six years and upwards at work earn from 11s. to 13. per week' (75). In 1905 'the board withdrew the subsidy as they concluded that the place was not suited for basket-making' (76). The basket industry site is now part of the Connemara National Park and the pre-fabricated building which accommodated the industry functioned until recently as a dance hall, a short distance west of Letterfrack village. Among those employed in the industry for periods ranging from two to over six years were W. Daly, T. MacDonald, G. Connolly, M. Hare, M. Martin, P. Coyne, M. Kearney, M. Mee, P. Connolly, P. Gibbons and J. Kearney (77) (Plate 9).

PLATE 8

Basket Industry at Shancoleir.
Courtesy of the National Library of Ireland.

PLATE 9

Employees of the Basket Industry at Shancoleir.

Courtesy of the Historical Library, Religious Society of Friends, Swanbrook House.

OVERVIEW

The most significant economic and social patterns emerging in Iar Connacht during the second half of the nineteenth century reflected those experienced at national level. The change in land proprietorship from large landowners to the small farmer was perhaps the most notable. The change in ownership was mainly facilitated through the allotment of available lands by the Land Commission and the C.D.B. The reallocation of lands led to an increase in the number of medium size holdings and together with the area's location and landscape proved more favourable to livestock production than to crop production. This in turn led to an increase in the number of livestock in Clifden Union.

During this period serious efforts were made to improve the productivity of the land in particular by large land owners who took up residence in the area during the nineteenth century. While property holders such as the Ellis's, the Eastwoods and Mitchell Henry would have been the principal people involved, small farmers continued to contribute to land improvement primarily through cultivation. Throughout this period, the dearth of roads and safe piers continued to hinder the development of non agricultural industries such as fisheries, quarrying and basketmaking in the area.

The overall trend in population during this period was one of decline. The remaining population became concentrated in the vicinity of employment opportunities as at Kylemore, Addergoole and Letterfrack where many were employed as agricultural labourers or in the local basket making industry. Government Relief works continued to have a significant role in sustaining the local population and in developing the roads network during periods of distress.

The years 1851-1891 witnessed what could be regarded as the initial stages of the tourist industry in north west Connemara. The Bianconi Car was first introduced in the area in the mid-nineteenth century to provide transport from Galway to Clifden. The opening of the Galway to Clifden Railway line in 1895 was probably the most important communications development in the area at the time. It contributed to the commercial development of Clifden town and provided western shores with a more efficient means of transport for those wishing to leave or visit the area.

REFERENCES

1. R.F. Foster, *Modern Ireland 1600-1972* (London 1988).
2. B. L. Solow, *The Land Question and The Irish Economy 1870-1963* (Massachussetts 1971)
3. H. Coulter, *The West of Ireland* (London 1862),p.87.
4. Eibhlín Ní Scannláin, "Athrú Tírdhreacha i bPáirc Náisiúnta Chonamara agus an Cheantair Máguaird ó Thús an Naoú Céad Déag". 1988. (Unpublished) NUIG.
5. Congested Districts Board Reports Vol. x (1907), 57275A.
6. *Baseline Reports to the Congested Districts Board Part II*, (1892), p.6.
7. D.A. Grigg, *Population Growth and Agrarian Change A Historical Perspective* (Cambridge 1980).
8. Griffiths Valuation Clifden Union (1855): K. Villiers-Tuthill *Beyond the Twelve Bens. A History of Clifden and District 1860-1923* (Galway 1986): J.A. Lidwill, *A Seagrey House The History of Renvyle House* (Galway 1986).
9. Foster, op.cit.
10. Tully Cross Guild, *Irish Countrywomen's Association Portrait of a Parish, Ballynakill, Connemara* (Galway 1985).
11. B.L. Solow, *The Land Question and the Irish Economy 1870-1963* (Massachussetts 1971).
12. Ibid.
13. Ibid.
14. Villiers-Tuthill, (1986), op.cit.
15. Ibid.
16. E.O. Somerville and V. Ross,*Through Connemara in a Governess Cart*, (London 1893), p.47.
17. Congested Districts Board, Reports Vol X (1907), 52691.
18. D.A. Gillmor, *Agriculture in the Republic of Ireland* (Budapest 1977), 43.
19. 6" Ordnance Survey Maps (1839 & 1969 eds.) Sheets 9, 9a, and 23.
20. Congested Districts Board, op. cit.
21. *Ireland Distress Maps* General Map (1889) 16 k 23 (7) N.L. Manuscripts.
22. Congested Districts Board, op. cit., 52691.
23. Ibid., 53053.
24. Ibid., 53047.
25. W.L. Micks, *An Account of the Constitution, Administration and Dissolution of the Congested Districts Board for Ireland from 1891-1923* (Dublin 1925).

87

26   Congested Districts Board, op.cit., 52896.

27   Ibid., p.57275(a).

28   Gillmor, op. cit.

29   H. Coulter *The West of Ireland* (London 1862), p.84.

30   Ibid., p.95.

31   Rev. J. Denham Smith, *Connemara Past and Present* (Dublin 1853), p.34.

32   J.H. Ashworth, *The Saxon in Ireland or the rambles of an Englishman in search of settlement in the west of Ireland* (London 1851), p.36-37.

33   National Archives Outrage Reports Mr. Eastwood's Correspondence A 357/177 1850.

34   Ibid.

35   A.I. Shand, *Letters from the West of Ireland 1884* (London 1885), p.123.

36   Ibid., 124.

37   R. D. Crotty, *Irish Agricultural Production its Volume and Structure* (Dublin 1966), p.84.

38   Nì Scannláin, op.cit.

39   L. Kennedy, Regional Specialisation, Railway Development, and Irish Agriculture in the nineteenth century, in J.H. Goldstrom and L.A. Clarkson (Eds.) *Irish Population, Economy and Society* (Oxford 1981), pp.174-193.

40   Ní Scannláin, op.cit.

41   Ibid.

42   Congested Districts Board, op.cit., 57275(a).

43   Ní Scannláin, op. cit.

44   D. Fitzpatrick, 'Irish Emigration 1801-1921' in *Studies in Irish Economic and Social History 1* (Dundalk 1984), p.19.

45   Ní Scannláin, op.cit.

46   Congested Districts Board, op.cit., 52691.

47   Baseline Reports (1892), op.cit., p.4.

48   National Archives Manuscripts 16K 21 Relief Works Ordnance Survey Maps,   1891.

49   Congested Districts Board, op.cit., 53008.

50   T.P. O'Neill,'Bianconi and his Cars' in K.B. Nowlan (ed.), *Travel and Transport in Ireland* (Dublin 1973), p.83

51   *P. Flanagan, Transport in Ireland* 1880-1910 (Dublin 1969)

52   W.B. Hartland, *Wayside Ireland* (Cork 1895), p.40.

53   J.H.Ryan, The Galway and Clifden Railway in *The Irish Builder Vol XL111*, No. 1022, July 17 (1902), p.1315-1317.

54   Congested Districts Board, op.cit., 54034.

55   Ryan, op.cit., p. 1315.

56   Hartland, op. cit., p. 32.

57   Ryan, op. cit., p. 1315.

58   Ibid., p. 1315.

59   Ibid., p. 1315.

60   Ibid.

61   Flanagan, Op. Cit. (Dublin 1969), p.172.

62   Villiers-Tuthill, (1986), op.cit., 113.

63   W.R. Hughes, *Sophia Sturge A Memoir* (London 1940).

64   Ibid., p.49.

65   Ibid., P 64.

66   Ibid., p.57.

67   Ibid., p.57.

68   Ibid., p.51-52.

69   Ibid., p.64.

70   Ibid., p.58-59.

71   Ibid.

72   W.J.D. Walker's *Report to the Congested Districts Board on the Basket Industry at Letterfrack* (1897), p.4.

73   Congested Districts Board Report (1907), op. cit.

74   Hughes, (1940), op. cit.

75   Walker, (1897), op.cit. p.3-4.

76   *Congested Districts Board Report* (1907), op. cit.

77   Walker, (1897), op. cit., p8.

Northwest County Galway underwent many changes in population, land proprietorship, agricultural practices and the development of communication networks during the nineteenth century. During much of the first half of the century Iar Connacht was largely isolated due the nature of the landscape, to a lack of roads and undeveloped harbours. The combination of these factors encouraged a subsistence economy and its associated practices to flourish and delayed the processes of change. As in many areas in Ireland, the small farmer and labourer population increased rapidly prior to 1841. Small farmers leased their holdings from the landlords and in turn subdivided their holdings in an effort to support the increasing population. The occupiers of a townland generally lived in cluster or clachan settlements and shared the land and amenities

PLATE 10

Commemoration Service for the Famine dead in Ballynakill graveyard, 1998

Courtesy of Padraic Lyden

together with the work and farm implements. Due to the poor returns from farming and high rentals many were forced to seek additional work in labouring, fishing, kelp making, illicit distillation and relief works.

Living conditions in north west Galway were already depressed prior to the Great Famine. Many landlords were experiencing financial difficulties and absenteeism was commonplace, resulting in little or no financial aid being available to their tenants. The workhouse in Clifden was opened during the height of the famine in 1847 and was soon overcrowded. Auxiliary workhouses, fever hospitals and outdoor relief centres were established in some areas as temporary measures in order to relieve the pressure on the workhouses. During 1847, the area was visited by members of the Religious Society of Friends. Their reports on the distress witnessed by them led to the arrival of James and Mary Ellis at Letterfrack. The Ellises' work saved many from the workhouse and provided the population with a basis for future development. More generally, road and harbour construction were among the main employment opportunities for the able bodied during this time. It is evident that the population living in close proximity to the sea were no better positioned to survive the famine than those further inland. Due to the poor fishing seasons experienced prior to the famine and the famine itself, many were forced to pawn or sell their tackle and boats in order to buy food.

The population continued to decline at D.E.D. level throughout the second half of the nineteenth century, although increases occurred in some instances at townland level. In the case of Letterfrack, where the population increased between 1881 and 1891, this may be attributed to the establishment of the Industrial School in 1887. Employment opportunities virtually dictated settlement trends in the area throughout the second half of the nineteenth century. It is clear that people concentrated close to relief and employment opportunities. The further development of roads also encouraged changes in settlement patterns from the clachan to a ribbon pattern.

One of the most significant changes to take place during this period was the transfer of land proprietorship from the landlords to the tenants. This again was a slow process and was mainly accomplished in the early twentieth century. The size of holdings also increased resulting in the largest increases occurring in holdings in the 30-50 acre category at the close of the nineteenth century. Farmers were now concentrating on livestock production and, in particular, sheep production. Land ownership also provided the sense of security and independence they so needed having experienced the capricious nature of their situation during the great famine. The change in land tenure provided a major incentive for agricultural improvement and Iar Connacht was established as a livestock (sheep in particular) production region.

The development of roads and the opening of the Galway to Clifden Railway in 1895 made north west Galway more accessible to tourists, thereby developing the tourism industry which was first serviced by the Bianconi cars. Towns such as Clifden greatly benefited from these developments resulting in tourism being one of the area's most lucrative industries today.